Table of Contents

1

Acknowledgements

Robin Rheeder

My gratitude goes to the Nommo Gallery in Kampala and Emanuel Mutungi, the director, who hosted the **Uganda at a Glance** photographic exhibition. It was from this competition that most of the photographs in this book were compiled.

Thanks also go to the judges of the competition: Dr Andrew Yiga, Mr Ifee Francis Xavier, Dr Nathan S. Senkomago, Mr Kalundi Serumaga and Mr James Tumusiime for their support in providing me with the majority of photographs used, and knowledge imparted on Uganda, my thanks also go to Paul and Jane Goldring, John Gibbons and Volker Riehl, for advertising the photo competition and providing us with the editorial. I thank the *New Vision* and the *Monitor* newspapers.

I would like to also thank my husband and travelling companion, Ian, for his support, photographic skills and good advice.

Finally, my continued gratitude goes to all those who gave me assistance, especially James Tumusiime, the managing director of Fountain Publishers, Pat Haward, David Isingoma, Tom Tibaijuka, Gustav Gonget and all Fountain Publishers' staff.

Sam Kalema

Uganda at a Glance:

Edited by: Robin Rheeder
Designed By: Gustav Gonget
and Peter Mwebembezi
Project Coordinator: David Isingoma

First published 2002 by
Fountain Publishers Ltd
Fountain House,
Plot 55 Nkrumah Road
PO Box 488
Kampala, Uganda
Tel: 256-41-259163 / 251112
Fax: 256-41-251160
Email: fountain@starcom.co.ug

Text and maps © – Fountain Publishers
Maps by Juliet Nsiima

Uganda at a Glance

Facts on Uganda

Uganda is a country of exceptional scenic beauty. The British wartime Prime Minister, Winston Churchill, could not hold back his opinion of this beauty and duly named the country the "Pearl of Africa."

Uganda is a landlocked country, which lies between the two East African Great Rift Valleys. It is crossed by the equator and is almost the same size as Great Britain or Ghana.

It shares her borders with Kenya, Sudan, Rwanda, Tanzania, and the Democratic Republic of Congo (formerly Zaire). It lies between the East and Central part of the great African continent.

Some of the magnificent scenery to behold, as will eventually be seen in pictures in this book, include snow-capped mountains, rolling plains, thick tropical forests, semi desert areas as well as tracts of thinly sparsed vegetation.

The country is plush green throughout most of the year, due to regular rainfall. The country has a substantial amount of natural resources, fertile soils and sizable mineral deposits.

Agriculture forms the most important sector of the economy, employing over 80% of the work force. Generally, industries form 17% of the sector, social services 40% while the rest of the economy relies on agriculture.

Lakes, rivers, swamps and other water bodies cover more than a third of the country. A greater part of Lake Victoria (48%), lies in the country. The rest of the lake is shared between Kenya and Tanzania.

Lake Victoria is the world's second largest freshwater lake while River Nile, whose source is in Uganda and covers over 4000kms, is the world's longest river. Other lakes include Albert, Edward, Kwania, Kyoga and Bisina.

Country name: Uganda

Area size: 241,139 sq km

Capital: Kampala

Major towns: Jinja, Entebbe, Masaka, Mbarara, Mbale, Fort Portal, Soroti, Lira and Gulu, among others. Entebbe is the country's International Airport town. There are 56 administrative districts or towns throughout the country.

Population: 24.6 million (2002 census)

Average annual income: Equivalent of US$310

Languages: English is the official language; Swahili and other Bantu languages, dominated by Luganda. There are over 30 different languages.

Religion: Roman Catholic, Protestant, Muslim, Greek Orthodox. Many other new ones are generally Pentecostal Christian churches.

Monetary Unit: Shilling. One US dollar buys the equivalent of 1800 shillings (August 2002).

Natural resources: copper, cobalt, hydropower, oil, limestone, salt and timber. Most of the land is used for arable farming. Agriculture is the backbone of the Ugandan economy.

Life expectancy: 44 years for men; 46 years for women.

Main exports: coffee, cotton, tea, fish and fish products, tobacco, maize, beans, pyrethrum and vanilla. New non-traditional exports are in the process.

Climate: Tropical, mainly rainy with two dry seasons. The northeast is semi-arid.

Terrain: mostly plateau with ranges of mountains

Time zone: GMT plus 3 hours

International dialing code: +256

Internet domain: ug

Weights (measure): metric

Welcome to UGANDA

If you turn these pages carefully and slowly you may absorb the true meaning of each image, depicting the beauty of this extraordinary country called Uganda. Each one is a snapshot of our time, each paragraph telling a little story, as we move into the 21st Century.

You are holding in your hands a document of great beauty and importance. Will it gather dust on your bookshelf, or will it always remain handy on your coffee table as you begin to weave a real magical mystery tour?

What makes this coffee table book different from others, is that Ugandans have taken the majority of photographs — both amateur and professional. So this book is Uganda - as seen through the eyes of the people.

The first thing that strikes you on arriving in Uganda is how lush and green and tropical it looks. The "Pearl of Africa" is certainly an exception to most African countries plagued by famine and drought. The people are also extremely polite and friendly, welcoming you at every opportunity.

Uganda's charm lies in its intimate landscapes, diverse people, unusual wildlife and compact travel circuit. This country is extremely fertile, and is covered in lush cultivation and dense luxuriant rainforests. Uganda is not a large country by African standards, but it holds some of Africa's best kept secrets. So read on to discover more about this magical country .....

Robin Rheeder

Uganda road network and tourist attractions

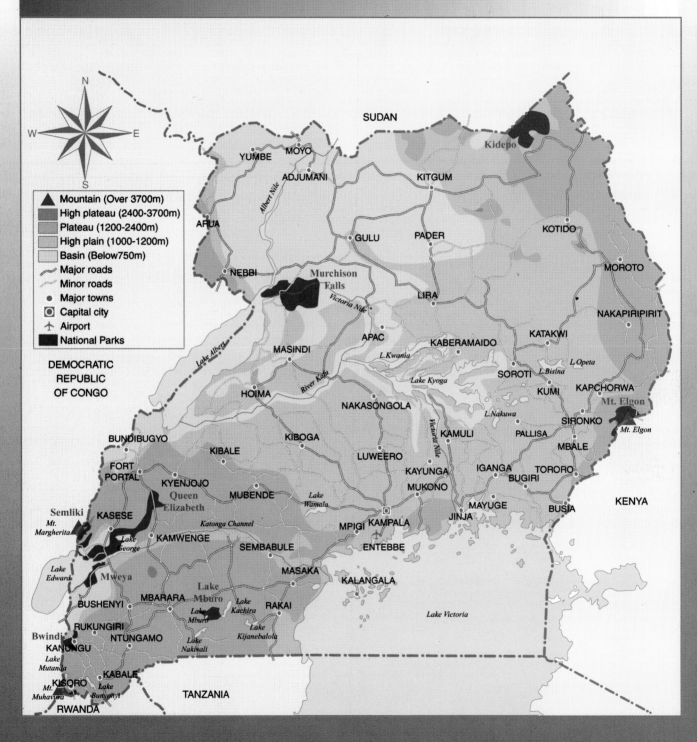

Introduction

Uganda lies astride the Equator covering an area of approximately 240,000 square kilometres, between the eastern and western ridges of the Great Rift Valley. It is a small landlocked state. Most of the country is over 1,000 metres in altitude with mountainous regions in the southwest and northeast. It is bordered in the north by Sudan, the east by Kenya, the south by Tanzania and Rwanda, and in the west by the Democratic Republic of Congo (originally Zaire).

The Rwenzori Mountains on the Congo border form the highest mountain range in Africa, the highest point being Margherita peak. The Virunga Mountain range in the southwest and Mount Elgon in the east are volcanic. Some 20% of Uganda's surface area is covered in water in the form of the Great Lakes: Lake Victoria (the second largest freshwater lake in the world), Lake Edward and Albert as well as other smaller lakes. The great Nile River, which is the longest in the world and whose source is in Uganda, courses through the landscape on its journey through Sudan and Egypt to the Mediterranean Sea. Most of Uganda is covered in lush vegetation except for the semi-desert northeastern region.

Uganda enjoys a fairly temperate climate with little variation. The temperatures range from 20ºC to 28ºC and the humidity is fairly high in some areas. Temperatures are generally moderated by altitude. The warmest climate occurs on the plains east of Lake Albert, while the lowest temperatures recorded are on the glacial peaks of the Rwenzoris. There are two rainy seasons, March to May, and mid-September to November. The vegetation ranges from dense rainforests, to grasslands, high altitude moorland, arid savanna and marshy wetlands.

Richard Gampp

Two young boys with their trusted old black bicycle standing on the Equator. The Equator crosses Uganda

Nikki Grant

Dawn breaks over Lake Victoria from Ggaba towards Port Bell, near Kampala, the capital city, also known as the city of seven hill.

A dead tree stands in Kidepo National Park landscape on the edge of the border with Sudan.

The average population of Uganda, at the time of writing, is estimated at about 22 million with an approximate growth rate of 3.5 % per annum. The majority of Ugandans live in the south and west of the country and 85% of the population eke a living off the land.

The official language is English (although it is a second language for most Ugandans). Uganda is one of the most heterogenous countries in the world and over 33 native languages are spoken in different parts of the country. Many Ugandans also speak some Kiswahili, which grew and spread into East Africa via the Arab slave traders. Christianity is the most widespread religion and there are also many Muslim converts.

Uganda has a free market economy and a democratically elected government. Although Uganda suffered at the hands of previous dictators such as Milton Obote and Idi Amin, since President Yoweri Museveni came into power, the economy has grown by 5%-7% per annum.

The volcanic soils on mountain sides are very fertile and much of the land has been utilised for agriculture which is the backbone of the Ugandan economy. The population earns a living from subsistence farming with coffee and tea being major exports; and cotton, tobacco and sugar being minor exports. Fish exports have of late become a leading foreign exchange earner. Groundnuts, maize, beans, sorghum and millet have emerged in recent years as cash crops for the peasant farmers. Other major industries include tourism.

Copper (the most valuable of Uganda's minerals since the pre-independence days) and small amounts of gold, tungsten, tin, lead and wolfram are extracted in the southwest. Salt deposits near Kasese have long been mined on a small scale, and brick clay supports a brick-making industry in the south.

Uganda has 10 national parks. Tourism, formerly a leading foreign-exchange earner, is struggling back on its feet. However some of the once numerous wildlife species almost disappeared between 1972 and 1990 due to poaching and unwanton slaughter by trigger-happy soldiers who shot at wild game both for target practice and food.

Since 1990, however, wildlife has slowly started to recover, and although you won't find the vast and variety of herds of game that typify Kenya and Tanzania, game parks still have a certain charm to them and they are a good eco-tourism resource. Uganda is certainly the easiest country from which to observe primates, such as gorillas, chimpanzees and many species of monkeys. For example, about 300 out of the 600 gorillas now left in the world are found on the Ugandan side, with the rest staying in Rwanda and Congo. It also has some of the best white-water rafting opportunities in East Africa, with the rapids of the River Nile below the Owen Falls Dam in Jinja.

A fisherman casts his net to catch the bountiful fish in Lake Victoria. Nile Perch now forms a huge chunk of the country's catch, which is also a popular export to Europe.

A Historical Perspective

There are no written records of events in Central and East Africa prior to the mid- 19th Century, and since history, by definition, relies upon written records, it is difficult to give an accurate account of what happened before this time.

What we do know is that between 1650 and 1850 there was much rivalry between the kingdoms of Bunyoro-Kitara, Buganda and Ankole. This took the form of cattle raiding and attempts by each faction to acquire more territory.

By the mid-19th Century, the Buganda kingdom stretched west from the Victoria Nile almost as far as Mubende, Ankole covered about 10,000 square kms between Katonga and Kagera Rivers while the Toro Kingdom occupied an area north of Katonga. Bunyoro-Kitara (which in the 17th Century had been the most powerful kingdom), was reduced to a quarter of its former size, retaining the Nile as its northern boundary.

In 1852 King Kamurasi seized the throne of Bunyoro. This coincided with the arrival of Arab traders from the north, who led many raids on the Luo kingdoms of Acholi up in the north.

In 1862 the first Europeans namely, John H. Speke and James Grant reached Bunyoro-Kitara. They were welcomed at Kamurasi's court. Speke was on a

National Bank of India, Kampala in the 1940s (now Stanbic Bank).

mission to 'discover' the source of the Nile. A few years later the big-game hunter and explorer, Sir Samuel Baker and his wife, arrived in the area. The missionaries from Europe followed shortly afterwards. Radical changes took place in the kingdom, and when Kamurasi died in 1869, Chwa Kabalega succeeded him. He was one of the greatest rulers with political and military reforms that have been compared to Shaka in Zululand, Southern Africa. The combined efforts of Govenor Generals Baker and Gordon did little to discourage Kabalega's empire building.

In the mid 19th Century, the first Arab slave traders arrived in Central Africa from the east coast of Mombasa. The regional power at the time was Buganda Kingdom ruled by Kabaka Mutesa I from Mengo near Kampala. At this time the Buganda clans were being influenced by the Arab traders' Islamic faith, rival French Catholics and British Protestants. Mutesa's court became a beehive of religious rivalry. When Mutesa died, his son Basanamula Mwanga took the throne and under a Muslim adviser, he ordered the execution of Bishop Hannington and 50 Christian converts, many of who suffered a horrible death of being burnt to death on a spit.

For the next period, more religious rivalry ensued and many European powers were eager to get their hands on the fertile kingdom of Buganda. In 1893 Sir Gerald Portal arrived in Kampala and raised the Union Jack over Old Kampala Hill. He signed a formal treaty with the unwilling but resigned Mwanga. Buganda's chiefs received British protection in return for freehold rights in land for themselves.

By the end of the 19th Century, the Uganda Protectorate included Buganda, Bunyoro, Ankole and Toro. British rule began in 1900 and continued for the next 52 years. Although colonisation had some positive aspects for Uganda, the arrogant and short-sighted British administrators sowed the seeds of future tragedy, even though they may have been unaware of it, at the time.

A regal Sir Frederick Muteesa II cuts a cool pose in all finesse while seated on the throne at Mengo.

Below: The King of Buganda, Kabaka Ronald Muwenda Mutebi II.

Uganda's first anti-colonial party, the Uganda National Congress (UNC), was founded in 1952 and the first serious plea for independence came from King Sir Frederick Muteesa II of Buganda, who asked that Buganda (alone) be granted independence. The governor, Sir Andrew Cohen, accused Muteesa of being disloyal to the British crown and exiled him to Britain. In 1959 the Uganda People's Congress (UPC) was formed by Milton Obote and at last they won the elections by a clear majority leading Uganda to independence on October 9, 1962. The first Obote government ruled from 1962 to 1971. Obote still recognised Kabaka Mutesa II who was first President as head of state. Tension between Obote and Mutesa culminated in the constitutional crisis in 1966 whereby Obote stripped Mutesa of his presidency. Obote sent his troops to the royal palace at Mengo which stormed the palace in a fight with Muteesa, then torched and razed the palatial residences down. Muteesa clambered over the palace's perimeter wall fence and escaped into exile to London through Burundi. Over 2,000 Buganda supporters of the king were loaded into trucks and jailed. Some were thrown into the Murchison Falls, while others were buried in mass graves. Obote declared a state of emergency and made himself an President of Uganda.

In January of 1971, Obote flew to Singapore for the Commonwealth leaders, conference. He left behind Idi Amin, the commander of the Uganda Army who was being asked to account for $4 million that had been stolen, and the murder of Brigadier Okoya and his wife in Gulu. It was then, that Kampala was shattered by the news of a military coup on January 25, 1971. Idi Amin took over power in Obote's absence.

Idi Amin's reign of terror extended from 1971 to 1979. He hailed from the north of Uganda and was born of a Muslim father and Christian mother. He had, during colonial times, quickly ascended through military ranks, and in 1966, he was second in command of the Uganda Army. After the constitutional crisis, Obote promoted

A young Premier Apolo Milton Obote with Sir Wilberforce Kajumbula Nadiope, who was the Kyabazinga of Busoga and Uganda's first Vice President at independence in 1962.

him to top military position. It was in fact Amin who gave the orders to murder 2,000 of the Kabaka's Buganda supporters, and co-ordinated the mass detentions of political rivals that followed the banning of the Democratic Party (DP) in 1969.

The first omen of things to come was when, in 1972, Idi Amin had expelled all Asians from Uganda, taking over their businesses, money, possessions which he dished out to his cronies. This eventually proved to be an economic disaster, but at the time, Amin won further support from most Ugandans who had resented the dominance and success of Asians in the business sector.

Amin slowly and secretly purged the army of its Acholi and Langi soldiers who were the majority, and by 1973, he had murdered 13 out of the 23 officers who had held high-ranking positions. In addition, eight out of 20 members of Obote's 1971 cabinet were killed and four others fled into exile. During the eight years that Amin was in power, about 300,000 Ugandans were killed by him or his agents (under the guise of the State Research Bureau). Many of them were tortured to death in horrific ways. He targeted any person or group that he perceived as a threat, and dealt with them ruthlessly.

Idi Amin's unpopularity with his own people grew and then he finally overeached himself by declaring war on Tanzania in 1978. A number of Ugandan exiles joined forces with Tanzania and retaliated by driving him out of Kampala and into exile in Saudi Arabia where he still remains today. Ironically, many Ugandans regard the seven years that followed Amin, to have been as bad, if not worse, than the years that preceded it. There were a couple of stand-in presidents until the lead up to the main elections. The rival political parties were the DP led by Paul Kawanga Ssemogerere, the UPC still led by Milton Obote, and a new party, the UPM (Uganda Patriotic Movement) led by Yoweri Museveni. The elections were rife with corruption and intimidation, and although it was initially announced that the DP were on the brink of victory (suggesting an anti-Obote sentiment), the edited results of the election saw the UPC triumphant, despite overwhelming evidence that the elections had been rigged.

Museveni and his people felt cheated and in 1982 they formed the National Resistance Movement (NRM) operating from Luwero. They began a guerrilla warfare against Obote's government. Obote's response was to invade the Luwero Triangle killing civilians by the thousands in massacres, which exceeded even Amin's.

Idi Amin doning his army uniform. Clearly visible are all the army ranks he acquired during his reign as the president of the Republic of Uganda.

Tito Okello, commander of the army, suggested that Obote negotiate with the NRM to stop the killings, but he refused. In July 1985, Okello took over the government in a military coup, and for the second time in his career, Obote was forced out by the commander of his own army. The NRM tried negotiations with Okello during talks in Nairobi, but after these broke down, Museveni returned to the bush. On January 26, 1986, the NRM besieged Kampala. Okello surrendered and Museveni was sworn in as the new President of Uganda - the seventh head of state in as many years.

So, in 1986 Museveni took charge of Uganda, a country worn out and brutalised for many years, and he initiated its slow recovery. He appointed a broad-based government, re-established the rule of law, appointed a

The Omugabe of Ankole Kingdom, Sir Charles Gasyonga II, inspecting a guard of honour composed of askaris in the 1960s. The kingdom has not been reinstated.

Human Rights Commission, allowed unrestricted freedom of the press, and asked for the return of Asians and other exiles. He encouraged foreign investment and tourism, and this has resulted in an average growth rate of 5-10% over the last decade. Another thing which gained him popularity was the restoration of Uganda's four traditional kingdoms in 1993. The son of Mutesa II, Ronald Muwenda

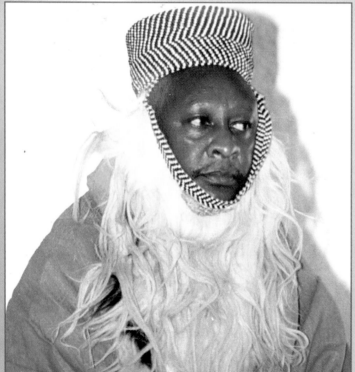

The King of Bunyoro, Omukama Soloman Gafabusa Iguru.

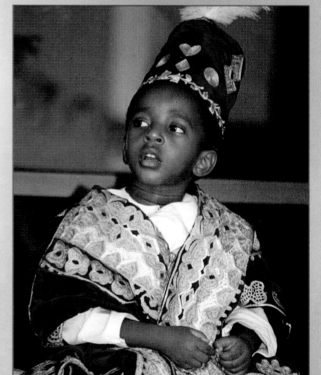

The Child King of Tooro, Omukama Oyo Nyimba Kabamba Iguru.

14

Peter Busomoke

President Yoweri Museveni with American First Lady Hillary Rodham Clinton during the Clintons' visit to Uganda in 1998.

Mutebi returned to Uganda after 20 years, having been educated at some universities in the United Kingdom, to become the 36th Kabaka of Buganda. In March 1994, voters elected a constituent assembly, which approved a new Constitution in 1995. This extended Uganda's non-party system of government for at least five years. The presidential elections finally took place in May 1996, and Museveni won with an overwhelming majority compared to his competitor, Paul Ssemogerere.

Another referendum in 2000 endorsed the Movement type of Government to continue and elections held in 2001 returned Museveni as the president for the second and last time.

Slowly but surely, peace and stability are returning to Uganda. It seems as though the "Pearl of Africa" is regaining its lustre, and it can truly be asked, 'Where might Uganda be today, without Museveni?'

Tourist & Beautiful

From gorgeous mountains of the Rwenzori, through game-packed savannas of the west and central Uganda, a rich cultural heritage, wonderful beaches of Kampala to the stunningly beautiful Bujagali falls of the east of Uganda.

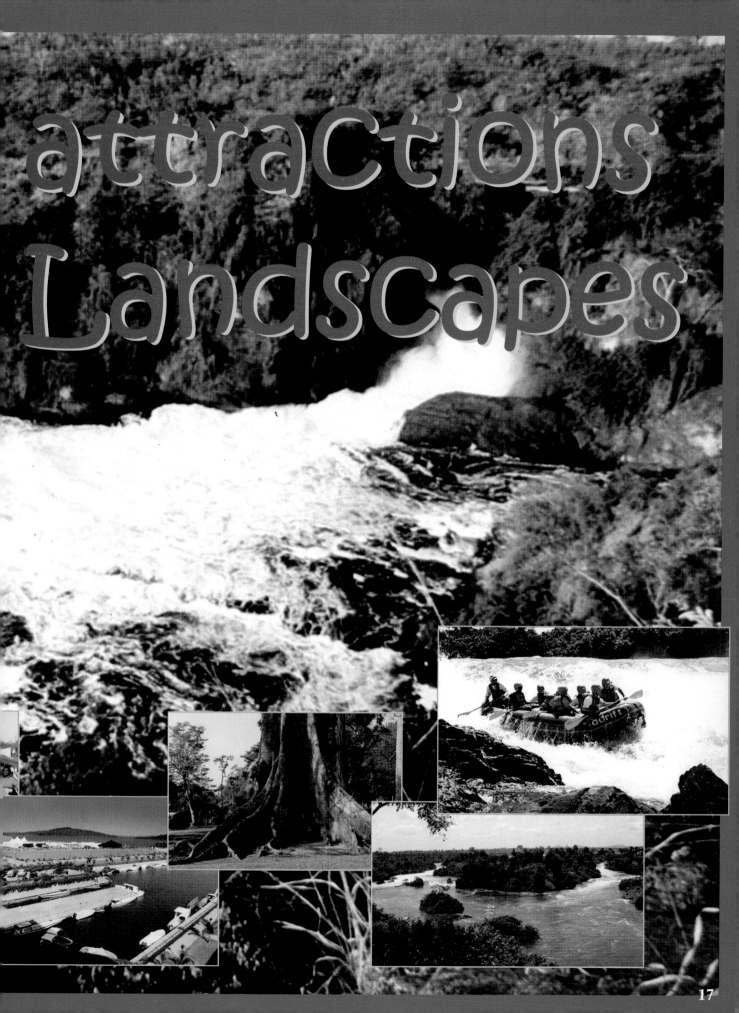

attractions
Landscapes

Kampa

Matthias Mugisha

The evergreen city of Kampala

Kampala is Uganda's capital and largest city. The name comes from the Luganda words for 'hill of antelopes" because in the old days, Buganda kings used to graze their impalas on the slopes of one of the hills now known as Old Kampala, which is the original site of the city. It is the nation's industrial, financial and commercial centre. The city has road and rail connections to the rest of the country and to the Indian Ocean through Kenya. Port Bell, 12 kms away on Lake Victoria and the Entebbe Airport, 34 kms to the south, are the two centres that serve the city.

Kampala is a processing centre for agriculture and livestock and it is where Makerere University (established in 1922) is located.

Sam Kalema

Kampala at sur

la city

Matthias Mugisha

The site for the capital was chosen by Lord Frederick Lugard, as headquarters for the British East Africa Company in 1890. Kampala was declared the capital of Uganda in 1962.

Just like the legendary city of Rome, Kampala is known as 'the City of Seven Hills'. These seven historical hills on which the city was founded are: Old Kampala, Mulago, Kibuli, Kololo. Makerere, Lubaga and Namirembe. These hills developed their own identities with Lubaga, Namirembe and Kibuli becoming the headquarters of the three main religions; Roman Catholic, Protestant and Islam respectively.

Nakasero and Kololo became prime sites for administrative offices and residential areas. Makerere (much later) evolved into a university campus and Mulago, a site for health institutions with the building of Mulago Hospital.

A bird's eye view of a modern swimming pool at the Sheraton Kampala Hotel

Peter Busomoke

The bustling Kampala taxi park, which handles more than a million commuters everyday. The ubiquitous "matatus" (mini-bus taxis) will ferry you to any part of the city, as well as other major towns upcounty. It is a cheap and convenient form of transport, although somewhat hazardous.

19

Kampala

by night

Kampala Golf Course along Kitante Road

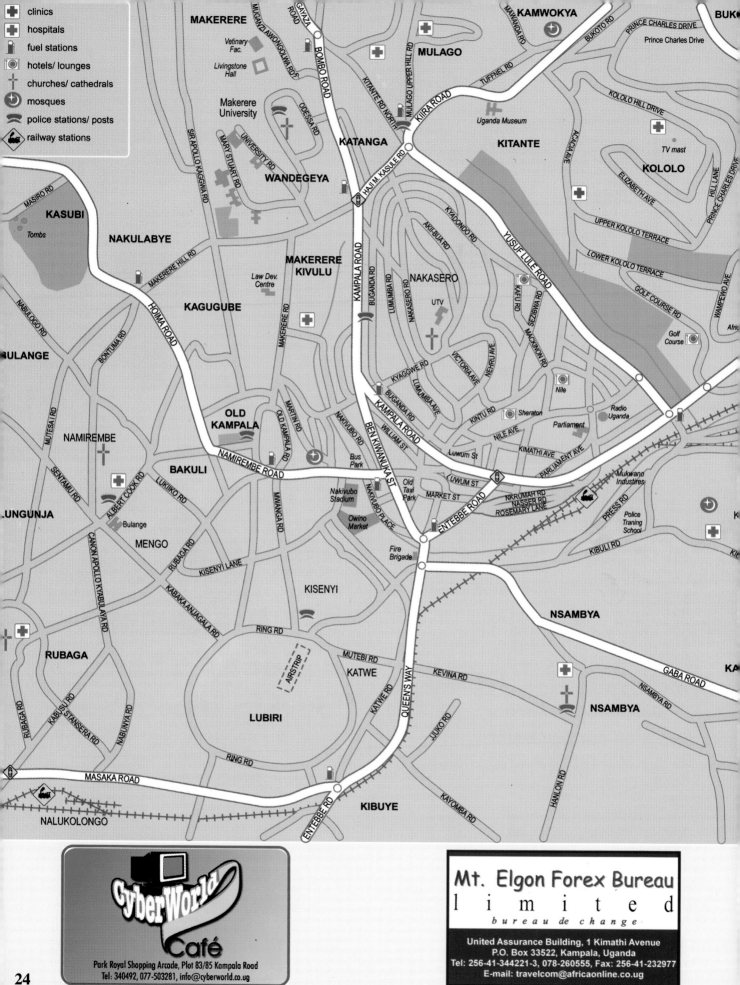

Map of Kampala

Map Labels

NAGURU
NTINDA
NTINDA
NTINDA RD
AIRSTRIP
KATALI
Oscar Industries
NAGURU AVE
KATAMO RD
ESTATE RD
NAGURU RD
Spear Motors
To Jinja
Naguru Housing Estate
Management Advisory Centre
NAKAWA
Makerere Business School of Commerce
MBUYA
UMA Show Ground
Vatican Embassy
Police Station
Conboni Missionaries
Lugogo Stadium
NEW PORT BELL RD
4TH ST
3RD ST
2ND ST
ST
Forestry Dept
KISWA
SPRING RD
LL RD
Sewerage disposal
5TH ST
Former CMB
USTRIAL AREA
SALMON RISE
6TH ST
FARADAY RD
7TH ST
Cattex depot
LUTHULI RISE
Shell depot
KIBIRA RD
BUGOLOBI
Radio Transmitter
Nakivubo Channel
KULUBYA CLOSE
Radio Mast
PRINCESS ANNE CLOSE
LUTHULI AVE
NAMUWONGO
NAMUWONGO RD
KIWULERIZA
KISUGU RD
To Port Bell
KISUGU
KAWEMPE
NAKAWA
RUBAGA
CENTRAL
BARNABAS RD
TANK HILL RD
MAKINDYE
TANK HILL
Gaba Rd
Water tanks
KAMPALA REGIONS
KANSANGA

Sheraton Kampala
HOTEL
Ternan Avenue, P.O. Box 7041, Kampala, Uganda
Phone: (256) 41-344591/6, Fax: (256) 41-256696
E-mail: sales@sheraton.com

Fazec

SAM'S RESTAURANT

25

Chris Pennington

Namirembe Cathedral is the architectural hallmark of the Church of Uganda. There are graves of some famous missionaries and Baganda notables in a cemetry right outside the church's entrance.

Bahai Temple, an architectural wonder, nestles in luxuriant, rolling gardens on Kikaya Hill, near Kampala. The inner sanctrum is all one room with several doors leading to it from all sides.

View of the Kibuli Mosque and Lake Victoria in the distance.

Namugongo Catholic Martyrs' Shrine, located 12 km. outside Kampala, commemorates the killing of 22 Ugandan martyrs on the orders of King Basammula Mwanga in the 1890s.

27

The main building of Makerere University, one of East Africa's finest institutions for higher education. It has recently celebrated 75 years of existence.

William Kazoora

Kasubi Tombs, probably the largest royal hut in Africa, bears the remains of three Baganda kings and some of their regalia. Elderly women keep all-day and all-night vigils at the tombs as the kings' "wives".

Eddie Kitayimbwa

"Urban Culturescape" – this interesting sculpture is found in the Sheraton Hotel gardens.

Richard Gamp

A colourful display of hand made stools for sale on the roadside.

Richard Gamp

Nakasero market in the city centre where anything from fruit and vegetables to poultry and beef, basket ware and papyrus woven mats and carpets can be bought.

Henry Bongereirwe

MANDELA NATIONAL STADIUM

The modern Nelson Mandela Stadium at Namboole on the Kampala-Jinja Road on the outskirts of the city is a world-class stadium. Opened in January 1999, it holds up to 40,000 spectators at a time. (Photo: Henry Bongyereirwe)

STADIUM MANAGEMENT COMM CONGRATULATES UGANDANS ON THE OFFICIAL OPENING OF MANDELA NATIONAL STADIUM

MADE IN CHINA

Time for real action: Athletics competition going on in Nambole National Stadium. Inset (above) is football match.

Sam Kalema

Taking you around Kampala

The endless lines of vehicles on Kampala streets

Lake Victoria, Entebbe and the enchanting Ssese Islands

Lake Victoria is the largest expanse of fresh water in Africa, about the same size as Ireland. The explorer, John H. Speke was correct in his belief that the Nile flowed out of Lake Victoria. The major towns on Lake Victoria are Kisumu (Kenya), Mwanza, Bukoba and Musoma (Tanzania) and Jinja, Entebbe and Port Bell (Uganda). It is the primary protein food source for many Ugandans. Small fishing villages along the shore live off the huge predator Nile Perch, the tasty Tilapia and the tiny Omena fish.

The Ugandan side of the lake is characterised by many small and large islands, with long finger-like peninsulas. Numerous papyrus swamps reach deep into the shores of the mainland, and parts of the lake are covered by water hyacinth, although the menace has now abated.

Fishing is a popular sport on Lake Victoria. Tilapia are fun to catch on light tackle, but the angling emphasis is on the Nile Perch. Specimens of over 200 kgs at

Nikki Grant

"Caught out in a shower ..." three-year-old Nkumwa 'sits it out', at Ngamba Island Chimp Sanctuary.

A view of Lake Victoria petering out in the distance between the hills and valleys of Mpigi District.

33

A local fisherman strains to hold up a massive Nile Perch that he has netted on Lake Victoria, from his simple wooden fishing boat.

this giant fish have been caught in nets, although the rod and line record is 114 kgs. These game fish are normally caught by trolling deep-sea lures or rapalas 8-10 metres below the surface.

The small town of **Entebbe** lies about 35 kms from Kampala on the banks of Lake Victoria. It is the site of Uganda's only international airport. The excellent Botanical Gardens offer good bird-watching opportunities and close-up sightings of the black-and-white colobus monkeys as well as numerous exotic plants introduced towards 1900.

You can also pay a visit to the Uganda Wildlife Education Centre (also known as the zoo) to see some of the rare animals and birds, in Uganda.

Paul Goldring

Hues of orange and pink light are cast on fishermen by the setting sun, as they gather their nets and start the long paddle home.

Addie Kitayimbwa

Entebbe International Airport received instant recognition in 1976 because of the "Raid on Entebbe" incident. An Air France plane, flying from Israel, was hijacked by Palestinian terrorists and forced to land at Entebbe. A group of Israeli paratroopers staged a daring surprise rescue mission, launched from Nairobi, and managed to free the hostages.

Fishing trips off the shores of Entebbe to the nearby cluster of islands are a popular excursion. So is the trip to the Chimpanzee Sanctuary on Ngamba Island.

This was opened in early 1999 and was largely the work of Debbie Cox who works for the UWEC and has done a great deal of research to protect the endangered apes.

20-odd habituated chimps, all of which are orphans, roam freely around the island. They come back to the viewing platform twice a day for their morning and afternoon feeding, offering people fantastic close-up sightings.

These gregarious African grey parrots are indigenous to Uganda.

These islands are lush and filled with bird-life, including pink-beaked pelicans. Otters are often seen in the area, and occasionally a small school of hippos too.

One of Uganda's relatively undiscovered treasures are the group of 84 Ssese Islands. This cluster of islands is about 55 kms southwest of Entebbe. The people of Ssese are said to be the friendliest in Uganda. Tropical rainforests extend down to the clear, warm waters and sandy beaches with rocky outcrops. It is an ideal destination for casual rambling. Traditionally, the Ssese islands are inhabited by a few small fishing villages.

Richard Gamp

A view of the Botanical Gardens in Entebbe. Established over 100 years ago, it contains specimens of both local and exotic plants.

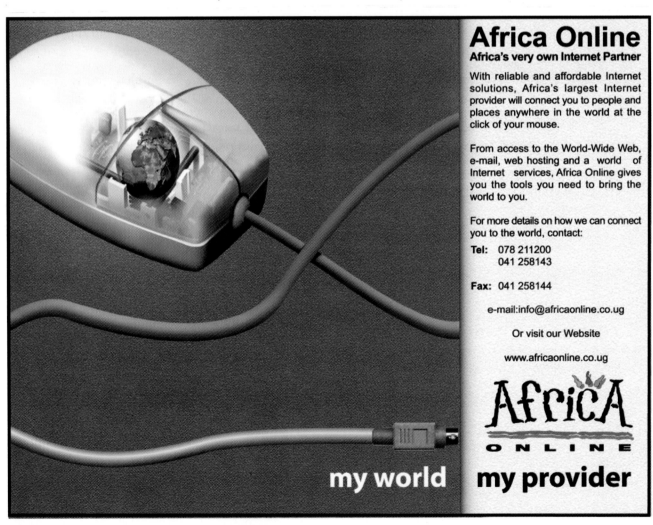

Dramatic blue and white skies contrast against a lush and undeveloped green landscape overlooking Lake Victoria and Entebbe.

The largest and most accessible island is Buggala, with its main town of Kalangala. Ferries run between the larger islands, and the best way to get around on any island is by foot or bicycle. Wildlife abounds with the shy Sitatunga antelope, black and white colobus monkeys and flocks of African Grey Parrots, Black and White Casqued Hornbills and Great Blue Turacos – indeed a birdwatcher's paradise!

A boat ride to Ssese islands

Portrait of a bicycle (used by Ugandans not only for transport, but also to carry heavy loads) on the Luku Ferry, Bukakata in the Ssese Islands.

Scattered like emerald gems in Lake Victoria are the cluster of Ssese Islands.

A keen angler struggles to get a grip on this heavy Nile Perch for a photo.

UGANDA
AERODROMES
MANAGED BY CIVIL AVIATION AUTHORITY

SUDAN

Under CAA Management

Designated entry and Exit points for International Flights

N.P National Park

DEMOCRATIC
REPUBLIC
OF CONGO

**ARUA

RIVER NILE

**GULU

**KIDEPO

PAKUBA

Murchison Falls
N.P

LIRA

MOROTO

LAKE ALBERT

LAKE KYOGA

SOROTI

MASINDI

Semliki N.P

Kibale N.P

Mt Elgon N.P

Rwenzori N.P

TORORO

KASESE

EQUATOR

ENTEBBE INTERNATIONAL
AIRPORT

KENYA

LAKE EDWARD

Queen Elizabeth N.P

MBARARA

Mburo N.P

LAKE VICTORIA

N

Bwindi N.P

KISORO

Mgahinga N.P

TANZANIA

UGANDA

CIVIL AVIATION AUTHORITY

Jinja, the source Mabira Forest

Jinja is the second largest town in Uganda, situated at the source of the legendary River Nile. It lies off the Nairobi-Kampala road, 82 kms east of Kampala. It is a humid, waterside town with thick vegetation and rattling with birds. The construction of the Owen Falls hydro-electric dam, in 1954, gave Jinja a tremendous advantage in attracting industries. One of Jinja's main tourist attractions is the actual source of the Nile at Owen Falls (now submerged by the Owen Falls Dam). There is a plaque that marks the spot where Speke stood and thus became the first European to sight the source of the river in 1862. Jinja also offers other recreational activities such as sailing on Lake Victoria, swimming, golf, tennis, fishing and of course the action-packed whiter-water rafting and kayaking on the Nile River.

The Bujagali Falls lie about 7 km upstream the river from Jinja. It is actually a series of large rapids. It is legend that if you keep your eyes peeled, you may see the spirit of, 'Mr Bujagali', who is said to float down the river on a barkcloth. Actually, you are more likely to see a local who astounds onlookers by swimming through the treacherous rapids holding onto a jerry can.

Sam Kalema

Bujagali falls on river nile at Jinja

Richard Gampp

# of River Nile and

He usually asks tourists to pay him 5 or 10 US dollars before he performs this dangerous feat. The Bujagali Falls are also known as a departure point for Adrift and Nile River Explorer's white-water rafting excursions. Unfortunately, it could become the site of a controversial dam and second hydro-electric plant, which will put to an end to all white-water rafting, and flatten out the beautiful rapids and waterfalls on that section of the Nile River.

The rapids of the Bujagali Falls is a pleasant tourist attraction, popular with picnickers and white-water rafters.

Richard Gampp

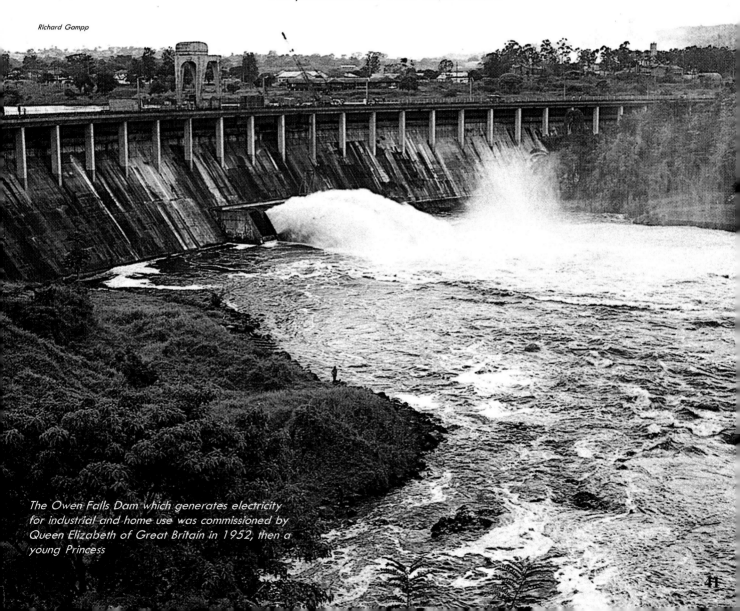

The Owen Falls Dam which generates electricity for industrial and home use was commissioned by Queen Elizabeth of Great Britain in 1952, then a young Princess

Kalagala rocks

Not far down the river after Bujagali is another set of rapids called the Kyabirwa Falls, which are also used by white-water rafting companies, and it is a good place to spend a few nights camping next to the Nile.

20 km from Jinja, towards Kampala, is one of the last of the best preserved sections of indigenous tropical forests remaining in south-eastern Uganda, namely Mabira Forest. It is abundant with bird life, butterflies and monkeys. Lovely walking trails and challenging mountain bike trails, make it an attractive spot for travellers. There are troops of red-tailed monkeys, and some colobus monkeys too.

Much of the forest is semi-deciduous. Tall canopies tangle among trees which are hundreds of years old.

Trails through the forest can be walked with or without a guide. Birds to look out for include the magnificent great blue turaco, the casqued hornbill and a variety of colourful sunbirds. A community camp site offers bandas and camping sites for people who wish to stay overnight in the forest reserve.

Kalagala rocks

The railway bridge across the Nile, which marks the entrance to Jinja.

Juma and Tootu — among the first Ugandan kayakers, having fun as they surf the waves on the choppy rapids of River Nile.

River Nile offers fantastic white-water rafting opportunities, and it is not for the faint-hearted. Here a raft bombs through the rocky rapids of Bujagali Falls.

Left: A huge "strangler tree" in the Mabira Forest, just one of many spectacular trees with an interesting root system.

Chris Billington

Robin Rheeder

A mountain-biking enthusiast enjoys cycling along one of the many trails that lead through the Mabira Forest.

Eddie Kitayimbwa

In the sunny open glades of the forest, particularly after the rains, you will see hundreds and hundreds of Uganda's beautiful and world famous butterflies flapping happily in the sun. Here a pretty specimen rests on a rain-speckled reed.

Kizito Mulumba

Southeast Uganda
Mbale, Tororo, Mt. Elgon and Sipi Falls

The pretty Sipi Falls are at an altitude of 1770 m. There are a number of camps and resorts in the area that offer you a spectacular view of the main waterfall. If you have a passion for adventure this is one place to visit.

The mesmerising Sipi Falls where the Sipi River gushes down a steep 50 metre cliff, on the footslopes of Mount Elgon.

Mbale is one of the more attractive towns in Uganda, and nearby Mount Elgon, is a major attraction for tourists, especially hikers. Mt. Elgon is a huge extinct volcano straddling the Kenyan border at an altitude of 4321 metres. Another popular spot is the Sipi Falls which lie on the foothills of Mt. Elgon. The small town of Tororo is only a few minutes drive from Malaba post on the Kenyan border. Its most noticeable feature is the huge Tororo Rock that juts out into the skyline. It is a steep volcanic rock that can be climbed in an hour or so, and on a clear day offers great views across Lake Victoria.

The Ugandan side bears the Mount Elgon National Park and was gazetted in 1993. The highest point on Elgon is Wagagai Peak which lies on the Ugandan side. The vegetation here includes distinct forest, bamboo, heath and afro-alpine areas – consisting of moorland with giant lobelias and groundsels. Mammals living in the park are the blue and de Brazza's monkey, black and white colobus, elephant, leopard, bushpig, duiker and sitatunga. The mountain also supports a rich variety of birds. Mt. Elgon is a relatively easy mountain to climb since no special skills are required, just general fitness. It is not high enough to be at any great risk of "mountain-sickness" (which is altitude related). Hikes can be organised from Mbale National Park Office or Budadiri.

There are several hiking routes for serious mountain climbers. The Sasa Trail is a four-day round trip from Budadiri to Wagagai Peak. You can also choose the five-day hike from Budadiri, which includes Wagagai and the hot springs. Alternatively you can ascend Elgon via the Piswa Route from Kapkwata, which is a less strenuous trail.

The pretty Sipi Falls are at an altitude of 1770 m. There are a number of camps and resorts in the area that offer a spectacular view of the main waterfall. You can also get a glimpse of Mt. Elgon's peaks, but only in very clear weather. Day hikes to the main falls are popular as well as three other smaller falls, and you can swim in the pools below the falls.

Within the national park is the Mt. Elgon Forest Exploration Centre. From here you can explore a series of day trails such as the Bamboo, Chebonet Falls and Ridge View Loops where you pass through exquisite areas of montane and bamboo forest and colourful wild flowers.

Golfers enjoying the outdoors on Tororo Golf Course, with Tororo Rock in the background. (Photo: Fred Kasoszi)

Villagers hitching a ride on a "matooke" truck near Mount Elgon. (Photo: Kirsten Durward)

Giant Groundsels in the Caldera region of Mnt. Elgon. (Photo: Brad Weltzien)

Kizito Mulumba

A Sabiny woman perched on a rock on the slopes of Mnt. Elgon, Kapchorwa. In the foreground is her home, a traditionally thatched hut with clay walls.

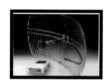

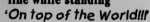

48

Brad Weltzien

Trekkers and porters hike through moorland vegetation of Smugglers Pass on Mt. Elgon.

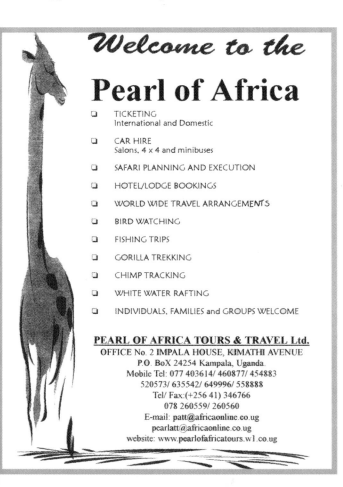
Kirsten Durward

Bottom right: The pretty Chebonet Falls, found on one of the circular trails leading from the Forest Exploration Centre.

Northern Uganda

Northern Uganda is quite distant and removed from the rest of the country. It is certainly an anomaly to the rest of Uganda with arid expanses rather than the typical lush greenness. The main attraction here is the Kidepo National Park, in the north eastern corner on the border of Sudan. It is isolated from the rest of the country by the arid Karamoja region, and not as well visited by tourists because of its remoteness. It is, however, one of Uganda's most fascinating destinations with rugged mountains and exceptional game viewing. The park is 1442 sq km and the highest point is Mount Marungole on the southeastern border. Kidepo has one of the most interesting faunas of any Ugandan National Park. The mountainous region is separated

An almost surreal backdrop, looking out over the Winway River Valley from Apoka Lodge, Kidepo National Park. Burchell's Zebra graze in close quarters to the lodge's verandah.

and the Kidepo Valley

The open savanna and Mount Irri beneath a blue sky, dotted with fluffy white clouds, in Karamoja, north eastern Uganda.

by the Kidepo Valley in the northeast and the Narus Valley in the southwest. The vegetation includes open and wooded savanna, patches of montane forest, miombo woodland, borassus palms, rocky koppies and riparian woodland. A total of 86 mammals have been recorded in this park, of which, 28 species are found nowhere else in Uganda. Some of the predators, rare to Uganda, are found here and include the black-backed jackal, African hunting dog, bat-eared fox, striped hyena, aardwolf, cheetah and caracal. An incredible 17 antelope species are also in Kidepo and endemic to the area are the Grant's gazelle, greater Kudu, Roan Antelopes, Beira oryx, Guenther's dik-dik and mountain reedbuck. The park also has a long bird checklist with mostly dry-country species and many raptors.

The northeast is home to Uganda's most unique ethnic group, the Karamojong. They are nomadic pastoralists whose love of cattle can be compared to that of the Maasai of Tanzania and Kenya. Some of these people have modernised into agriculturists, while others have remained the traditional hunter-gatherers. They speak various dialects of the Nilotic Karimojong language.

Other major towns in Northern Uganda include Lira, Gulu, Pakwach and Arua, while the towns of Soroti, Moroto and Kotido are found in the northeast. Arua is a relatively large town fairly close to the Congo border and 130kms northwest of Pakwach. It has a lively market with a large missionary and NGO/aid-worker presence. If you climb the hillsides outside town, you can view countryside for miles west over the Congo border, and to the east, River Nile. Lira, the gateway to the northwest is a pleasant little town and famous for it large numbers of fruit bats that can be seen congregating in trees in the park and parade grounds. Gulu is the largest town in northern Uganda and still bears the scars of civil war from the Obote and Idi Amin days. Pakwach is perched on the West Bank of the Albert Nile. As you enter the town, you cross the only bridge connecting Nebbi and the Arua districts to the rest of Uganda.

Soroti is midway between Mbale and Lira. Like Tororo further south, this large town lies beneath a striking rock formation which you can climb for views to Lake Kyoga and beyond.

Vincent Mugaba

A local woman goes about her daily chore of collecting firewood, in the town of Lira.

Mount Moroto bathed in the enchanting golden glow of sunset

W. W. Obote

Sunset over Kotido, a dry and arid landscape with cactus plants in the foreground and the jagged, rocky mountains on the horizon.

John Gibbons

A large herd of buffalo and some elephants living in harmony in the Narus Valley, Kidepo Valley National Park.

Sam Kalema

Smart Karimojong girls. Look at their traditionally decorated dresses

John Gibbons

A herd of eland in the Narus Valley, dominated by the typical rugged mountains that makes this region so unique and picturesque.

Paul Goldring

Murchison Falls, Budongo Forest and Surroundings

The "Devil's Cauldron"
of the Murchison Falls, where a huge volume of water
thunders through a relatively small gap, causing a spray of
mist to shoot up onto the air like a fine rain shower as the
water tumbles in a swirling pool.

The prehistoric-looking shoebill or whale-headed stork takes flight from the papyrus swamp using his incredible wing span.

Murchison Falls is the largest National Park in Uganda. Teeming with hippo, crocodile and bird life, the Victoria Nile launch-trip below Murchison Falls is considered to be one of Uganda's most exciting wildlife experiences. It is also one of the best places to spot the elusive shoebill stork which lives in the papyrus swamps. En route to Murchison is the Budongo Forest which has the region's largest wild chimpanzee population.

Masindi is the gateway to Murchison Falls and the Budongo Forest. The national parks office is found on the outskirts of this town with useful booklets and general information on the area.

There are two routes between Masindi and Paraa (the headquarters of Murchison Falls National Park). The advantage of the Bulisa route is that

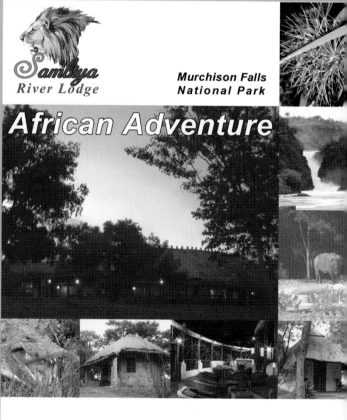

Elephants graze in the Queen Elizabeth Ishasho Sector

it is very scenic as you descend from the Rift Valley escarpment with views of Lake Albert.

Budongo Forest Reserve is the most extensive mahogany forest in East Africa and covers about 450 sq km. An estimated 900 chimpanzees live in the forest and chimp tracking in the early morning has become popular with tourists. More than 330 bird species have

The "launch trip" takes tourists upstream on the Nile River to the base of the Murchison Falls. A guide on-board points out the various wildlife and birdlife along the way.

been recorded, particularly rare forest species such as the blue-throated roller, dwarf kingfisher and grey-chinned sunbird. Budongo has one of the longest recorded logging histories worldwide, and thus makes an excellent site for studying forest regeneration.

Murchison Falls National Park covers 3840 sq km. The terrain is predominantly savanna, with some ironwood forests and borassus palm. The park is bisected by the Victoria Nile flowing west between Lake Kyoga and Lake Albert. The most striking feature is the 43m high waterfall, more notable for its raw power rather than its size.

Most of the Nile River funnels through a 7m wide gap in the rocks and comes shooting out the other side. If you have your own fishing tackle, there is good fishing on the banks of the Nile, below the falls with large and fierce-fighting Nile perch and tigerfish.

Although Murchison Falls National Park suffered from heavy poaching in the 1970s and 1980s it is slowly recovering and up to 76 mammals have been recorded in the park. Antelopes common in the area include the

Another view of the falls from a hiking trail, showing the Murchison Falls on the right

Jackson's hartebeest, Uganda kob, Defassa waterbuck and bushbuck. It is also a birder's paradise with 460 confirmed species. A ferry crosses the river taking passengers and their vehicles to the other side of the park. The popular launch trip from Paraa to the base of the falls is a must for all visitors. In addition to taking you close to the base of the falls, the scenery is beautiful with borassus palms, acacia woodland and mahogany trees. The game viewing from the boat is excellent: huge crocodiles, hippo, buffalo, waterbuck, kob, elephant, bushbuck and colobus monkeys. The birdlife is also stunning with goliath heron, saddlebilled storks, pied and malachite kingfishers and red-throated bee-eaters – just some of the species regularly seen.

The boat trip from Paraa towards Lake Albert is favoured by birdwatchers with the best opportunity to see shoebills anywhere in Africa. Most game drives originate from the Sarova Paraa Lodge and the strange ecosystem of borassus grassland begins near here. It is called a "fire climax community" brought about by constant burning and then browsing by elephants. This area probably used to be woodland and grasslands with just a scattering of borassus -which has now become the main vegetation in this region due to environment changes. It is also found in west and central Africa, and the Karamoja district of Uganda.

Chris Billington

A huge crocodile basking in sunshine on the banks of River Nile opens its massive jaws to bare razor sharp teeth to tourists who watch him from the safety of a launch trip boat.

A spectacular view of birds and hippos as you cruise on River Nile in the Murchison Falls National Park.

A wild chimpanzee climbs a tree in Budongo Forest. Some of these chimps have become so habituated that tourists have a chance at spotting them.

A solitary buffalo, one of the most dangerous animals in Africa, standing next to a borassus palm in the Murchison Falls National Park. Note the birds picking ticks off its back.

A brilliant African sunset over Lake Albert, truly God's country.

The sheer power of water showing at the top of Murchison Falls before it plunges through a 7 m wide cleft in the rocks, and shoots out the other side.

Fort Portal, Rwenzori Mountains and Semliki Valley National Park

Fort Portal is one of the prettiest towns in Uganda, situated westwards in the northern foothills of the Rwenzori Mountains. It is the capital of the Toro kingdom set in lush hills, tea plantations and with views across the mountains. The original fort named after Gerald Portal was built in 1891 and has now become the site of the golf course in town. It was built to ward off attacks from King Kabalega of Bunyoro Kitara and his guerillas. Sir Gerald Portal arrived in Uganda from Zanzibar to formalise the British protectorate of Uganda. Unfortunately he died of malaria a few months after the fort was completed.

The "Mountains of the Moon" (a romantic name for the Rwenzoris) astound visitors with their snow-covered peaks and are found on the Equator of all places. Experienced hikers and casual-day hikers will find it a thrilling experience to trek through spectacular vegetation and scenery, unique fauna and flora and ice-rimmed sculptures. The region is usually shrouded in mist, giving it an eerie but fascinating feel. Unlike most mountains in East Africa, the Rwenzoris are not volcanic. During the creation of

Richard Gampp

Rolling hills of green tea plantations are typical of the region surrounding Fort Portal.

Mount Speke and its glacier. This is the second highest mountain in the Rwenzoris.

Bujuku Valley and river in the rainforest zone on the lower slopes of the Rwenzoris.

r Riehl

Lake Kitandara, the highest glacial lake in the Rwenzoris. The water from this lake is sustained by the snow melting off Mount Stanley.

the African Great Rift Valley, these mountains (which are 120 kms long and 48 kms wide) were formed, and they run along the Congo/Uganda border. The Rwenzori National Park is 996 sq km. At the centre of the range is Mount Stanley (the third highest in Africa) and six snow-covered peaks.

The main attraction for climbing these mountains is not so much to reach the peaks and glaciers, but rather to enjoy the wonderful views and fascinating vegetation on the way up. Due to strange evolutionary patterns, the plant life here grows to huge proportions. Groundsel plants and giant lobelias tower above you.

The lower slopes support a forest zone with a variety of birds and mammals, including the golden cat, servaline, genet, elephant, chimpanzee, yellow-backed duiker and forest hog. At about 2500m the forest gives way to dense bamboo, and higher still is the open vegetation of heather and alpine with giant lobelias, groundsels and giant heather plants.

There is a network of trails but most people follow the loop trail which takes six or seven days to reach one of the peaks at an altitude of 4372 metres. It is also possible to do shorter 3-day hikes in the forested moorland zone.

North-west of Fort Portal lies the Semliki Valley and National Park. The park shares its unique ecosystem with the Ituri Forest which lies across the Semliki River in the Democratic Republic of Congo. It is made up of tropical lowland forest with diverse vegetation which is wetter and more dense than most. It is of particular interest to bird watchers, and almost 400 species have been recorded here. Some of the more unusual mammals that occur in Semliki are the pygmy antelope, flying squirrel and six different types of bats.

A popular tourist attraction is the cluster of hot springs at Sempaya. Not far from here, in the direction of Bundibugyo you can find pygmies, who traditionally lived a nomadic lifestyle – but have now settled in a village called Ntandi.

Volker Riehl

A giant tree groundsel in the afro-alpine region, with Mount Baker peeping out the top of the clouds in the background.

Stunning scenery and fantastic vegetation found around every corner when hiking in the Rwenzori Mountains.

A giant 'lobelia beguaerati' found on the slopes of the Rwenzoris. These plants grow to absurd proportions, sometimes 8 or 10 metres high.

The Jirikiti flower (local Luganda name) otherwise known as the red-hot poker tree flower, 'Erythrina abyssinica' – common in Western Uganda.

Some young girls having fun bathing in the Semliki River near Bundibugyo.

A view over the tranquil Semliki Valley in Western Uganda.

Western Uganda: Queen Elizabeth

Butyaba escarpments in Masindi district

The Kibale Forest is 766 sq km, situated southeast of Fort Portal and it is continuous with Queen Elizabeth National Park. This park is situated in a rainforest, interspersed with patches of swamp and grassland. It is a unique, moist, evergreen forest habitat and supports a high diversity of wildlife and flora. One of the prime attractions is tracking habituated chimpanzees. Kibale offers superb primate viewing, but it is not an easy place to see larger mammals which are also present. The elephants that live here are a special forest species, in that they are smaller and hairer than the savanna elephant. About 335 bird species exist in the forest, with a similar range to those

A curious chimpanzee with a bird's-eye view, perched on a broken tree top in Kibale Forest.

Kibale Forest and National Park

Ian Rheeder

The yellow grass of the open savannah leading down to one of the sparkling crater lakes near Mweya in Queen Elizabeth National Park.

found in the Semliki National Park. The altitude ranges from 1,590 metres in the north to about 1,110 metres in the south – and this contributes to the differing vegetation found in the park.

A short distance west of Kibale Forest is a field of 30 crater lakes, namely the Bunyaruguru Crater Lake field. They are the result of volcanic and geological forces that have shaped the landscape of western Uganda. Each of these beautiful lakes is a different shade of blue or green. You can go boating and swimming, and the birdlife in the area is abundant. Legend has it that the lakes were created by Ndahura, the first Chwezi king.

On the Congo border lies the Queen Elizabeth National Park. It runs from the base of the Rwenzoris in the north, down to the Ishasha River in the south. The park is also bordered by Lake Edward to the west, and Lake George to the north east as well as the Kazinga Channel which connects these two lakes.

Richard Gamp

A spectacular view of birds and hippos as you cruise on Kazinga in the Queen Elizabeth National Park.

Experience Nature while in

Uganda

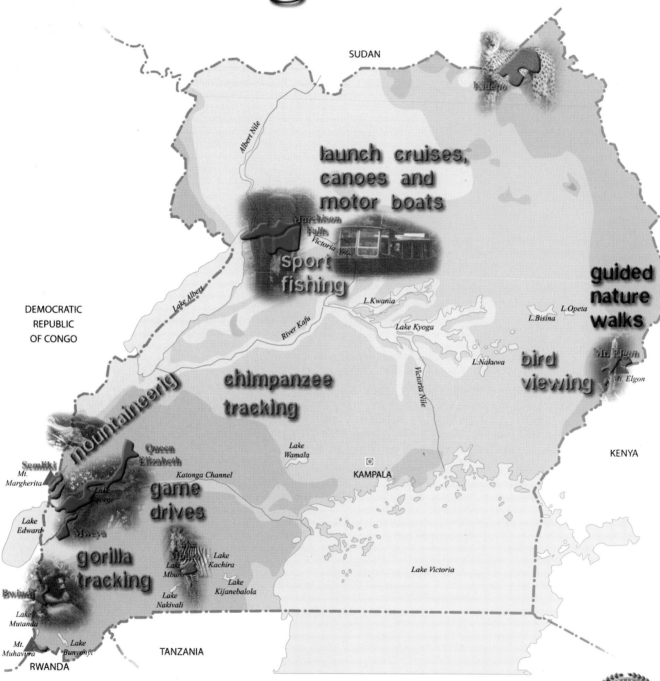

SUDAN

Kidepo

Albert Nile

launch cruises,
canoes and
motor boats

Murchison Falls

Victoria Nile

sport fishing

L.Kwania

L.Opeta

guided nature walks

L.Bisina

DEMOCRATIC
REPUBLIC
OF CONGO

Lake Albert

River Kafu

Lake Kyoga

L.Nakuwa

Mt. Elgon

Mt. Elgon

chimpanzee tracking

bird viewing

mountaineering

Queen Elizabeth

Lake Wamala

Victoria Nile

KENYA

Semliki

Mt. Margherita

Katonga Channel

KAMPALA

Lake George

game drives

Lake Edward

Mweya

Lake Mburo

Lake Kachira

gorilla tracking

Bwindi

Lake Mutanda

Lake Nakivali

Lake Kijanebalola

Lake Victoria

Mt. Muhavura

Lake Bunyonyi

TANZANIA

RWANDA

UGANDA WILDLIFE AUTHORITY

Headquarters: Plot 3 Kintu Road, Nakasero
P.O. Box 3530, Kampala, Uganda
Telephones: +256-41-346287, 346288, 346290, 346651
Fax: +256-41-346291, E-mail: uwa@uwa.or.ug, Website: www.uwa.or.ug

UWA

Krsten Durward

A shot of two young Defassa
waterbuck glancing over their
shoulders, on the road in Queen
Elizabeth National Park.

A lioness looking out for a meal at Queen Elizabeth National Park.

A healthy male lion scrutinises the photographer in Queen Elizabeth National Park.

Mining salt the traditional way in Katwe, Queen Elizabeth National Park.

Just outside Kasese lies this classic mountain landscape at the base of the Rwenzoris, overlooking the Margerita Hotel grounds.

The vegetation is diverse with savanna, acacia and euphorbia trees, large areas of swamp, the Maramagambo Forest and the Chambura Gorge. Ten sparkling crater lakes lie within the reserve. The most visited area for game viewing is north of the Kazinga Channel near Mweya Lodge. The less visited Ishasha sector is far south on the Congolese border around the Ishasha Camp.

Like most Ugandan parks, the wildlife suffered terribly from civil war and poaching in the 1970s and 1980s, but since stability returned to Uganda, animal populations have steadily increased. This park has a fantastic variety of animals, including 95 mammal species and 10 primate species. About 20 predators are found here, including the spotted hyena, lion and leopard. The buffaloes, which are common in the park, are often reddish in colour due to inter-breeding with a redder race of Congolese buffalo that lives in the rainforest. A total of 547 bird species have been seen in the park, and Mweya is probably the best place to go bird-watching for the scores of water birds on the Kazinga Channel. The riparian forest in Ishasha in the south, is also a good place to view more unusual species.

From Mweya camp, you can organise a launch trip on the Kazinga Channel, which offers wonderful game and bird-spotting opportunities. Wild chimpanzee tracking is possible in the Chambura Gorge.

Katwe is a small town south of the Rwenzoris on the shores of Lake Edward, facing Mweya peninsula. The main road to Katwe offers very good game viewing. Katwe is an odd little urban settlement and is strangely charming. It is beautifully located on a grassy rise with Lake Edward to the south and two saline craters to the north. Local salt extraction has gone on for a long time in Katwe, near Queen Elizabeth National Park.

Kasese is the main town connecting Kampala to Western Uganda. It lies at the foothills of the Rwenzori Mountains, 75kms south of Fort Portal. It has in one past years seen a fair amount of traffic due to being the main base for hiking and climbing in the Rwenzoris. Although the town itself is quite run-down, hot and dusty – this contrasts sharply with its beautiful setting at the base of the "Mountains of the Moon" – one of Africa's largest mountain ranges.

A worthwhile activity is a walk out to the Margherita Hotel or hiring a bicycle from the Saad Hotel and taking the 11km route out to Kilembe Copper Mines.

At sunset, shades of orange and gold fall across the Kazinga Channel with the

South Western Uganda: Lake Bunyonyi, Kabale, Kisoro and Mgahinga.

Kigezi region is located in the southwest corner of Uganda, one of the most attractive and distinctive parts of the country. The typical scenery found here is steep hills of terraced cultivation, giving off a patchwork effect. This region is extremely fertile because of the volcanic soil and ideal climate for cultivating crops. The largest town in the area is called Kabale, a friendly town where it is often said, that some travellers plan staying one night and end up spending a week. This town is often used as a base from which to visit mountain gorilla forests, or the sprawling Lake Bunyonyi, which is strewn with many pretty islands. The lake, about 6 km from Kabale, is very picturesque. You can take rides in dugout canoes, go for walks, watch spectacular birdlife and even camp on one of the islands.

This erratically shaped lake with many fingers, is 900m deep in parts. The weather is very cool, because it lies at an altitude of 2,000 metres.

Ian Rheeder

The cultivated landscape and terraced hills of Kabale District, near Kisoro with the Mgahinga Gorilla National Park in the distance.

Sam Kalema

The erratically shaped but picturesque Lake Bunyonyi.

75

A panoramic view of the Virunga Mountain range showing the peaks of Mt. Muhabura, Sabyinyo and Gahinga, and the terraced hills of Kigezi in the foreground.

The steep-terraced hills are covered in cultivation, as are most of the islands. Bunyonyi means, "place of little birds" – and it's not difficult to see why. You can also spot otters at a place called Kyabahinga. Close to the mainland is Far Out Island with a tented camp that is highly recommended. It is said to be safe to swim in the lake which is too cold to support the bilharzia parasite, and there are no hippos or crocodiles found here. Even the fish are very tiny, but the small fresh-water crayfish are worth feasting on.

Bushala Island is a community project set on a small tree-filled island in the middle of the lake. This is simply a 'top spot' – tranquil, filled with birds and commands beautiful views over the lake. You can stay in standing tents, or pitch your own. Monday is a market day, and it is quite amazing to watch hordes of dugout canoes coming from every direction, loaded

with their cash crops as they descend on Kyabahinga, near Kabale.

Kisoro lies at the base of the Virunga Mountains near the Rwandan and Congolese borders. It is often used as a base for visits to the mountain gorillas in Mgahinga National Park or the Djombo Gorilla Sanctuary in the Congo. The setting here is quite breath-taking, with hills rolling out in every direction and the volcanic peaks of the Virungas rising into the sky to the south. It is a wonderful area for day excursions and hikes, especially to Lakes Mutanda and Mulehe surrounded by mountains, and only a 6-8 kilometre walk from Kisoro.

Mgahinga Gorilla National Park is Uganda's smallest national park and also one of the newest. It borders Parc National des Volcans in Rwanda, and Parc

Blasio Byekwaso

The Gashijja Caves, near Kisoro, not only provided shelter for Stone Age people, but until recent times (1960s), were still being used by Batwa (pygmies) for shelter.

Ian Rheeder

The view across Lake Bunyonyi from the tented camp on Far Out Island.

National des Virungas in the Democratic Republic of Congo. The Ugandan side of the Virunga mountain range include six mountains, three active and three extinct peaks. The three extinct volcanoes lie within the park: Mt. Muhabura (4127m), Mt. Gahinga (3475m) and Mt. Sabyinyo (3645m). Mgahinga is an afro-montane tropical rainforest, including a montane forest belt, bamboo zone, an ericaceous belt (heather-type plants) and an alpine zone. There are also three large swamps in the park, namely: Rugezi, Kabiranyuma and Kazibakye. This park offers panoramic views over steep volcanic cones in the south, and the Bwindi hills in the north. Mgahinga is famous for gorilla tracking but strangely, these gorillas do not live in the park permanently. They move freely between Uganda and Rwanda. However, gorilla tracking is not the only attraction. The park offers other activities such as forest walks, day hikes to the three volcanic peaks and also caving, for example, the exploration to Garama and Gashijja Caves, near Kisoro.

Neatly terraced rows of cultivation, along the Kabale-Kisoro road.

The fascinating caldere 'Mother Earth Cooking Pot' crater, overlooking Lake Mutanda, just outside Kisoro, in South West Uganda.

78

Robin Rheeder

Mgahinga is situated within one of the most densely populated parts of rural Africa, surrounded by the terraced hills of the Batwa and Bafumbira people, who once were hunter-gatherers and are now keen agriculturists.

Young and energetic men ready to help you cross lake Bunyonyi

Blasio Byekwaso

A young gorilla, unfazed by tourists pops his head out the top of the foliage in Mgahinga Gorilla National Park.

Ian Rheeder

A banana plantation in Kisoro, surrounded by cultivated hills, and the dramatic backdrop - one of the mountain peaks in Mgahinga.

The Bwindi Forest and

Its not just a thick forest, it can also be fun after a long day of gorilla tracking.

Impenetrable
its Environs

Bwindi Impenetrable National Park is the third largest forest in Uganda. It lies on the Congo border at the edge of the western Rift Valley. It is a true rainforest, stretching over steep ridges and valleys, and is considered to be one of the most biologically diverse forests in Africa.

Tourism centres around gorilla tracking and more than half of the world's mountain gorilla population lives here. There are about 15 troops comprising an estimated 300 individuals. Much of the vegetation is similar to Mgahinga with a very dense, thick undergrowth – hence the name "impenetrable" making gorilla trekking very strenuous work. At the time of writing there were two fully habituated groups and a maximum of six visitors per group per day are allowed. It can take anywhere between two and

The magnificent forest gallery of the Bwindi Impenetrable National Park, in the foreground a hiker is geared to go gorilla tracking.

Spotting this family group of gorillas, including a silverback on the right and the female with babies (inset), makes the difficult trek all worthwhile.

Ian Rheeder

Above: National park trackers and tourists in search of gorillas in the Bwindi Impenetrable National Park.

six hours of a grueling trek to find the gorillas, and then you are allowed an hour's visit with them.

Bwindi has diverse vegetation with both montane and lowland forests, the Mubwindi Swamp as well as an extensive stand of bamboo. This rich ecosystem supports 93 mammal species and 10 different types of primates, including the mountain gorilla, chimpanzee, blue monkey, black and white colobus, red-tailed monkey, L'Hoest's monkey, Demidoff's galago bushbaby, baboon, potto and needle-clawed galago. Six antelope species occur, including bushbuck and five types of forest duiker. A total of 345 birds have been recorded, and this area is home to roughly 300 types of butterfly.

Blasio Byekwaso

The pretty Munyaga River waterfalls found on one of the hiking trails in the Bwindi Impenetrable park, National Park.

A pensive and yet alert gorilla, resting in the thick forest and bamboo vegetation in Bwindi.

In addition, 14 species of snakes can be found in Bwindi, 27 types of frogs, as well as many different chameleons, lizards, skinks and geckos. There are over 163 species of trees in the Bwindi forest, and some of the most significant being the fabulous Mahogany trees.

The park headquarters are at Buhoma, about 108 kms from Kabale. The drive to Bwindi is very pretty, passing villages, forests and beautiful tea plantations. The Buhoma community campsite is a delightful spot set on a slope of grass just outside the park gates. It faces the dense forest gallery, and makes you wonder how on earth you will track gorillas through there, but most people do manage

when motivated to come face to face with this fascinating animal.

Once again, Bwindi offers more than just gorilla trekking. There are five different trails ranging from 30 minutes to eight hours offering awesome scenery, monkeys and birdlife. One of the prettiest trails is the Waterfall Trail crossing the Munyaga River several times before reaching the thirty three-metre high waterfall. The bridges and forest vegetation on the way, look like something out of a storybook, resembling a landscaped garden of ferns, streams and waterfalls, rather than a wild and natural forest. The Rushara Hill Trail and Mzubijiro Loop offer wonderful views across to the Virunga Mountains.

Ian Rheeder

Another day ends as the soft sunlight flickers on the rolling hills along the road to Buhoma.

Paul Goldring

A tea-picker harvesting the crop on one of the lush plantations surrounding Bwindi.

fly Africa...
...fly AfricaOne

For reservations please call 344520, 346980, 078 261212 or your travel agent

AfricaOne
The Continents Airline

Lake Mburo National Park, Mbarara District and Environs

This 260 sq km park includes Lake Mburo and four smaller lakes, fed by the Ruizi River. Sitting at an altitude of between 1200 and 1800 m above sea level, with a low annual rainfall, makes it one of the hotter, drier parts of Uganda. Permanent and seasonal swamps connect the lakes. The park is mainly savannah with acacia trees, open grasslands, thickets, woodlands and wetlands. Lake Mburo is home to a wide variety of wildlife and birdlife, although it does not have all of the 'Big Five'. This area was originally used by the Bahima pastoralists for grazing cattle and goats. When it was gazetted as a national park in 1983, many pastoralists and local fishermen were forcibly removed. This caused a lot of dissent, but now with the creation of a community conservation unit, the local people have been included in boosting tourism and conservation, so that it involves and directly benefits them.

Ian Rheeder

The beauty of early morning, as the mist slowly rises off Lake Mburo.

A large herd of Uganda Kobs in Lake Mburo National Park.

A large herd of buffalo gathers in a clearing between the scattered acacia trees in Lake Mburo National Park.

The west side of the park has rugged hills and flat-bottomed grasslands, ideal for game viewing. The east side has undulating low hills and rocky outcrops. In Lake Mburo National Park you see some of the last remaining herds of impala, found nowhere else in Uganda. The park also supports herds of buffalo and Burchell's zebra. Other antelope include eland, topi, klipspringer, oribi and reedbuck. The lakes and fringes are home to plenty of hippo and crocodile, and in the papyrus swamps, the sitatunga. Predators are seldom seen, which makes this park ideal for walking safaris, provided you are accompanied by an armed ranger. You can also hire a wooden Ssese canoe for a tour of Lake Mburo and close-up encounters with hippo and crocodile. For bird-lovers, Mburo has 310

Lake Mburo is one of only two Uganda national parks where the Burchell's zebra still exists.

different species, and particularly interesting are the bare-faced lourie (go-away bird), the Ruppell's long-tailed starling and the black-bellied bustard.

Mbarara, a major town which is 4 hours' drive from Kampala, is the gateway to western Uganda. It is also an important agricultural area. Mbarara was the capital of the Ankole kingdom back in the 1500s, but in 1875 it fell into decline due to the rise of Bunyoro Kitara Kingdom as well as disease. The old Ankole capital still lies 2 km from Mbarara on the Fort Portal road. Another place of interest is the Nkokonjeru Tomb, 4 km west of the town, where the last two Abagabes (kings) of Ankole were buried.

Wilkins. E. Kyawe

The green, undulating hills in Ankole, Western Uganda. This is Ndeija sub-county at a place called "Nyamukana" in the Mbarara District on the Mbarara-Kabale Road.

Robin Rheeder

Lake Mburo National Park: savannah and acacia trees give way to the Mazinga Swamp, and on the horizon, the rolling hills of Mbarara District.

The meandering Kagera River, as seen from Katongelo hill, Kyebe sub country in the Rakai District. The Kagera River begins life in Rwanda, weaving across the plains before finally flowing into Lake Victoria. It is typical of the whole riverine system. The river and surrounding beauty make it an area worth discovering.

Nuwagaba. C. Tumusime

An unusual rock formation known as "Karegyeya Rock" in Ntungamo on the Ntungamo - Rukungiri road

Taste of Uganda
Recipes for traditional dishes

Jolly Gonahasa

Available in most book stores!

Wonderful People, Rich Cultural Heritage

Uganda is divided up into 45 districts as shown on the map (opposite), however, the six main co-operating districts are Acholi, Lango, Bunyoro, Buganda, Busoga and Ankole. There are over 30 ethnic groups that can be divided up into four broad linguistic categories: the Bantu, Atekerin, Luo and Sudanic. The country's name "Uganda" came from the ancient kingdom of Buganda.

The Bantu, who make up 50% of Uganda's total population, occupy the southern part of the country. They can be found in the districts of Kampala, Mpigi, Mukono, Masaka, Kalangala, Kiboga, Rakai and Mubende. The ethnic groups that are Bantu-speaking include the Baganda, Banyoro, Basoga, Bagisu, Banyankore, Bakiga, Bafumbira, Batooro, Bakonjo, Bamba, Batwa, Banyole, Basamia-Bagwe and Bagwere.

The Atekerin category, often referred to as the Para-Nilotics, the Lango or the Nilo-Hamites are found in northern, eastern and north-eastern Uganda. They originate from Ethiopia and include the Karimojong, Langi, Iteso, and

Mathias Mugisha

Portrait of a Ugandan woman, with a ready smile and friendly nature.

93

Meet the beauties of

ganda

95

Vincent Mugaba

Kumam.

The Luo group migrated from southern Sudan. They reside in the West Nile, northern and eastern Uganda. This group comprises the Acholi, Jonam, Alur and Jopadhola.

Lastly, the Sudanic group of the West Nile include the Madi, Ikebu, Lugbara, Bari, Metu and Kakwa. Although they originate from the Sudan, their language and culture have changed radically, and they have now become completely detached from their place of origin.

Over the years there has been a major cultural transformation. This has been due to colonisation, improved transport and communication links, urbanisation, education and religious influence. For example, the Arabs brought the Muslim

Three men dressed in traditional kanzus (white tunics) carrying a gift of meat to a bride's parents in Ggaba, Kampala.

Sam Kalema

Cultural dancers doing their Kiganda Bakisimba thing.

James Akena

A wooden carver puts final touches to a piece of furniture with intricate design depicting village life.

Sarah Johns

Vincent Mugaba

Little children share a light moment in the doorway of their home at Katwe, a slum in Kampala.

A man carries a gourd full of banana wine to a bride's home on an introductory ceremony.

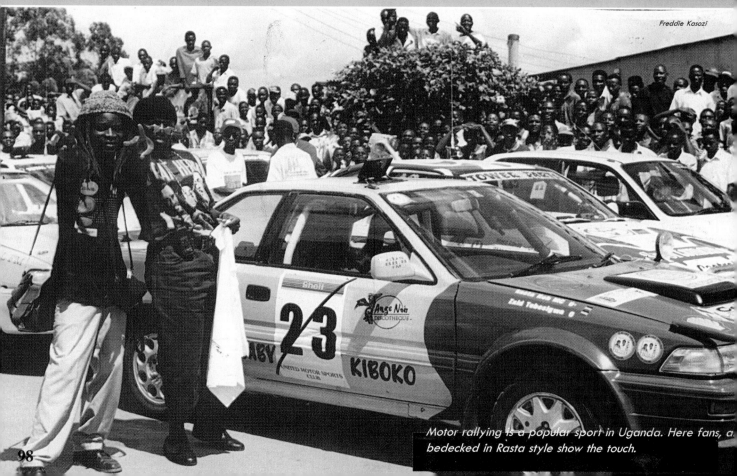

Freddie Kasozi

Motor rallying is a popular sport in Uganda. Here fans, bedecked in Rasta style show the touch.

Freddie Kasozi

Many newly founded radio stations use phone-in programmes and quizzes to lure listeners. Here CBS radio executives dole out goats and other gifts to winners shortly before Christmas.

Youths of Bbunga Trading Centre cheer
the photographer with a victory sign.

Muslim women and
their children walk for
Idd prayers at
Nakasero Mosque in
the city.
(Photo: Peter
Busomoke)

religion to Uganda and Europeans brought with them Christianity. Before this time, Ugandans' religion revolved around their ancestors, witchcraft and worshiping idols.

The custom of male circumsision is unique to the Bagisu. It is a mystery how this tradition originated. One story is that "Masaba" (the Bagisu hero ancestor) wished to marry a Kalenjin girl. Another theory is that someone had a complication with his sexual organ, and this resulted in a surgical operation to save his life.

Yet another legend states that circumcision was done as a punishment for seducing other people's wives. The Bagisu are a highly superstitious people, and before circumcision, the young boy is administered a herb called *idyanyi*. Circumsision is carried out twice a year, but only during leap years. Every male has to perform the ritual before he reaches puberty. Before the day, initiates walk around and dance for three days. Their heads are sprinkled with cassava flour and their faces are painted with *malwa* (millet beer) yeast paste. Friends and relatives, including girls, enthusiastically take part in the dancing ceremony. It is believed that once a boy is circumcised, he becomes a true man, or "Mugisu". On the day, the boys awaiting circumcision gather in a semi-circle. The circumciser performs each operation very quickly after which the teenager is wrapped in a piece of cloth and made to sit on a stool. Then he is taken

Sam Kalema

Performers of Ndere Troupe, one of Uganda's most famous dance troups in traditional western Uganda regalia and pan pipes.

Paul Goldring

Takeaways!! A boy selling sticks of barbecu[ed] liver to bus loads of passengers that pass on the Jinja Road. You can buy anything on [a] skewer from liver, dried fish to goat's meat.

Francis Kirya

Elderly traders from Namunyumya (in Busoga) blowing traditional horn instruments called "Bigwara".

Fishermen and fishmongers dealing soon after the catch is landed on one of many beaches around Lake Victoria.

Dancers from nothern Uganda perfoming Rarakaraka, one of Uganda spectacular dances.

A Sabiny woman in Eastern Uganda carrying a pile of firewood through the terraces of Mount Elgon. The Sabiny inhabit Kapchorwa District, which stretches from the cold heights of Mount Elgon to the hot plains of Karamoja.

Kizito-Mulumba

Uganda's Giant – John Paul Ofwono, one of the tallest men in Africa, measures at 7 ft 4 inches. He lives in Oyokolo village in Eastern Uganda, and is pictured here with his father and stepmother.

Charles Maloba

Vincent Mugaba

The Bamasaba circumcision dance, practised by the Bagisu of Eastern Uganda.

to his father's house and is hand fed, because he is not allowed to feed himself for three days.

The Karimojong are found in the Moroto and Kotido districts of northeastern Uganda. They fall under the Atekerin-speaking category of ethnic groups. They are pastoralists and have an intense love for their cattle. Cattle are a sign of wealth and are needed to pay the dowry when taking a bride. To this day a lot of cattle raiding goes on, especially between the Karamajong and their Kenyan neighbours. Many of these warriors have now

Some Karamojong elders cooling off in the afternoon shade.

Vincent Mugoba

A Karamojong maiden adorned with bright bead necklaces in Moroto.

Curtis Abraham

A Karimojong vigilante proudly displaying his gun.

Vincent Mugaba

The defiant grimace of a modern-day Karamajong warrior. The army beret and the marks on his chest show how many men he has killed.

neighbours. Many of these warriors have now substituted their spears for rifles. Some of the Karamojong have forsaken their traditional ways to become agriculturists while others are still hunter-gatherers and have moved from the dry plains to the mountains. The Karamojong are apparently something of an embarrassment to the westernized Ugandans since they are considered backward and move around half-naked. However, this is one of the aspects that makes them so interesting to the tourist or historians. They are one of the tribes that have been least influenced by westernisation and have retained most of their cultural heritage.

The Pygmoids: In Uganda these include the Bambuti and Batwa tribes. They are traditionally hunter-gatherers and live a nomadic lifestyle. Over the years, their lifestyles have changed, probably because there is no longer much scope for hunting and gathering. They often exist by begging or working for other tribes like the Bahutu and Batutsi. They are related to the pygmies of the Congo, the Koikoi San of South Africa and the Ndorobo of Kenya.

The Bambuti are found in Bundibugyo and Kasese in Western Uganda, in the tropical forests of the Congo River Basin. Their language is Kanambuti, which is apparently very complex and difficult to learn. Their average height is about 1.5 metres and they have a light brown skin and curly, wooly hair. Their huts are made of leaves and grass, with tiny entrances that require crawling into. These huts are temporary due to their nomadic existence. They wear belts with barkcloth attached, and brass-wire bangles. Sometimes they walk around stark naked, or very skimpily dressed.

Paul Goldring

Portrait of a Ugandan woman with a ready smile and friendly nature

Sam Kalema

Ugandan woman and her baby

The Banyankore are part of the Bantu group. They come from the old Ankole District in Western Uganda – which now comprises the present districts of Mbarara, Bushenyi and Ntungamo. The word Ankole was introduced by the British colonial government. The Banyankore originated from the Congo region. This society can be split up into the Bairu (agriculturists) and the Bahima (pastoralists). The two groups who speak the same language have a lot in common and recognise common ancestry. They used to depend heavily on each other. The Bahima would provide the Bairu with cattle products, while the Bairu would provide the Bahima with fruit and vegetables, especially local beer. So it was in both their interests to trade and exchange goods.

109

Uganda Ethnic Groups

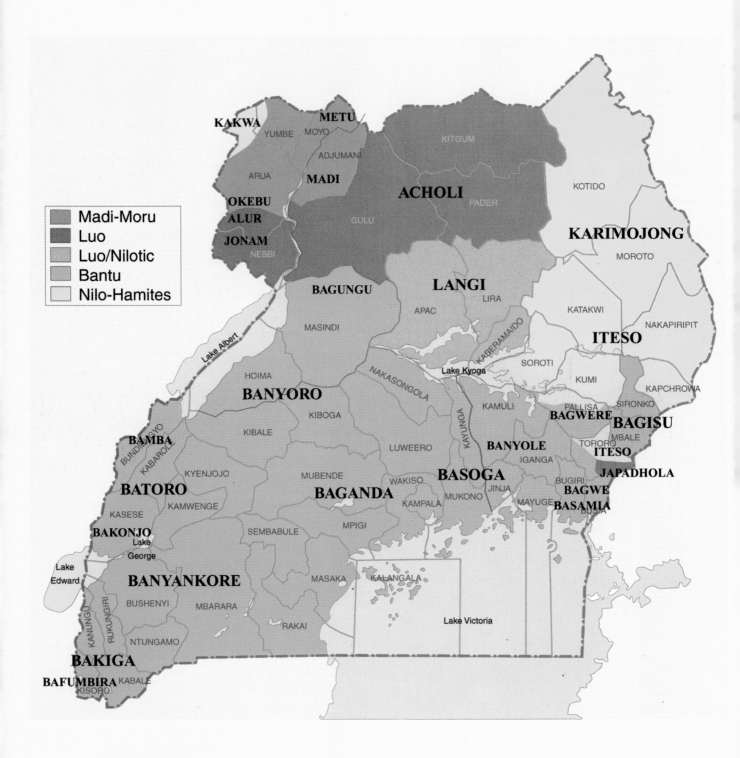

Legend:
- Madi-Moru
- Luo
- Luo/Nilotic
- Bantu
- Nilo-Hamites

KAKWA — METU — YUMBE — MOYO — ADJUMANI — ARUA — MADI — OKEBU — ALUR — JONAM — NEBBI — KITGUM — ACHOLI — PADER — GULU — KOTIDO — KARIMOJONG — MOROTO — BAGUNGU — LANGI — LIRA — APAC — KATAKWI — NAKAPIRIPIT — MASINDI — KABERAMAIDO — ITESO — Lake Albert — HOIMA — NAKASONGOLA — Lake Kyoga — SOROTI — KUMI — KAPCHROWA — BANYORO — KIBOGA — KAMULI — PALLISA — SIRONKO — KIBALE — BAGWERE — BAGISU — BAMBA — BUNDIBUGYO — KABAROLI — LUWEERO — BANYOLE — TORORO — MBALE — ITESO — KYENJOJO — IGANGA — JAPADHOLA — BATORO — MUBENDE — WAKISO — BASOGA — BUGIRI — BAGWE — KAMWENGE — KAMPALA — MUKONO — JINJA — MAYUGE — BASAMIA — KASESE — BUSIA — BAKONJO — Lake George — SEMBABULE — MPIGI — Lake Edward — BANYANKORE — MASAKA — KALANGALA — KANUNGU — RUKUNGIRI — BUSHENYI — MBARARA — Lake Victoria — NTUNGAMO — RAKAI — BAKIGA — BAFUMBIRA — KABALE — KISORO

Courtesy of E. R. M. Muslime

Two Karamojong young men photographed in 1956. The one on the left is attending to the other's head-dress. Physical appearances are of the utmost importance to this tribe and they dedicate a great deal of time to beautifying themselves.

Vincent Mugaba

A typical Karamajong homestead

Left: Langi tribesman with his spear. The Langi belong to the Lango family and come from the Apac District (formerly known as Lango District). Their traditional homeland was north of Lake Turkana, where they used to live alongside the Karamojong. Their origins stem from Abyssinia (present Ethiopia).

111

Sid Adams - Courtesy John Gibbons

Young Acholi girls from Northern Uganda in a traditional jig called Larakaraka.

Peter Busomoke

Peter Busomoke

The Acholi drummers and dancers.

Acholi men ready for the Bwola dance.

The Acholi are from northern Uganda. They live in the Gulu and Kitgum districts (formerly Acholi district). The traditional head-dress is made from many different types of feathers, including those of the ostrich. The dancers use leopard skins to adorn their waists and bang tunes out of calabashes struck by a handful of bicycle spokes.

Nubian women attending a cultural ceremony in Arua, West Nile, northern Uganda. They are part of the Madi-Moru group.

A pygmy family in Bundibugyo - the head of the family with his bow and arrow, and the mother suckling her baby.

Richard Gampp

A Muhima man smoking a pipe.

Nikki Grant

A women's cultural group warms up to the rhythmic drum beat at Buhoma, hear Bwindi Impenetrable Forest and National Park.

The unfazed face of a wise old man peering into the distance near Lake Katwe salt extraction works, Queen Elizabeth National Park.

Portrait of a young Karamojong wearing a traditional head-dress and lip plug in Moroto in 1950. Scarification of the body forms part of the Karamojong culture of adornment.

These people are related to the pygmy tribe, although the ones pictured here are a little more westernised than the traditional pygmies found in the Congo basin. The Batwa dancers pictured here have probably intermarried with other tribes in the Kisoro area, but are easily recognised by being much shorter than other Africans.

The Bakiga come from Kabale and Rukungiri Districts. Due to overpopulation, some of them have migrated to other parts of Uganda. Most of the Bakiga are hard-toiling subsistence farmers, growing millet, beans, peas, Irish potatoes and sorghum. They also make beer and non-alcoholic beverages from sorghum. Some keep cattle, sheep and goats, while others make pottery. The Bakiga are excellent blacksmiths who will forge spears, hoes and knives from any scrap of metal.

A group of Batwa dancers performing an ecstatic dance in Kisoro, South West Uganda. (Photo: Courtesy of E. R. M. Musiime)

A grand old Mukiga blacksmith wearing the charms of his trade around his neck in Rwamuchuchu in Kabale. (Photo: Courtesy of E. R. M. Musiime)

Richard Gampp

A man carries his produce of carrots to the market.

James Sempa

Paul Goldring

A peasant farmer proudly shows off his huge cabbages in the terraced hills of Kisoro.

A cultural dancer works himself in a frenzy during a church ordination at Kinanira - Kisoro.

James Sempa

Fishermen in the Kigezi Hills, south west Uganda with wicker baskets used for trapping fish, which are then stuck onto long skewer sticks and smoked.

Richard Gampp

Left: Uganda's unique Ankole long-horned cattle — linked to the Bacwezi and Bahima. These cattle produce superb beef and their horns are of an extraordinary length. Some local industries polish and carve the horns into luxury belts, hair combs and other ornamental jewellery.

Richard Gampp

The long-horned cattle are gradually being replaced by the exotic cattle that have higher yields of milk.

Richard Gampp

A young Muhima herdsboy looks after his family's cattle.

A traditional Hima hut, constructed from grass. It is specifically designed to be temporary, because these pastoralists are constantly on the move to find new pastures to graze their cattle.

A Munyankore headsman in traditional attire, tending to his Ankole cattle.

A Munyankore woman in traditional attire.

Children use a stool to pick Jack fruit from a Jack fruit tree (Artocarpus heterophyllus). Originally from the East Indies, this tree bears large fruits with rather an unpleasant smell when ripe. However the seeds and pulp are very sweet and greatly relished by most Ugandans. Jack fruit can be seen growing wild throughout Uganda.

ohn Mary Kabigyoma

Alex Kirinda Kakaine

These beautiful baskets are finely woven from selected grasses and straws by communities of women in Ankole and Tooro. They keep meals of millet bread and cassava warm.

Thatched granaries used for storing dry grain, cassava and sweet potatoes.

Sam Kalema

Traditional handmade mats and baskets common in central Uganda

Gorgeous birdlife and big game

Being a small country, and one that has suffered years of civil war - Uganda's wildlife is not as plentiful as that of its East African neighbours, Kenya and Tanzania. However, it does have a great diversity of animals and incredible rainforests that support a wealth of wildlife, particularly primates. Uganda is one of the most accessible countries in Africa to see mountain gorillas, chimpanzees as well as ten other types of monkeys and even the wide-eyed bushbaby. The "Big Five" are still found in Uganda although in smaller numbers, and you can certainly see elephant, leopard, buffalo and lion. However, rhinoceros are now extinct but they are to be re-introduced by the Rhino Fund.

Uganda is one of the finest birding countries in Africa. When visitors arrive at Entebbe and Kampala, they are struck by the abundance of birds in gardens and forests. It has serious "birders" doing double flick-flacks with over 1,000 species recorded. This is more than what is found in South Africa and Tanzania, which are much larger countries than Uganda, and excellent bird-watching destinations in their own right. Included in the checklist are migratory species from Asia and Europe. Uganda is particularly rich in West and Central African forest birds, found in Budongo, Kibale, Semliki, Bwindi, Kalinzu and Maramagambo. Even when walking down the

Paul Goldring

A group of keen bird-watchers in Bwindi Impenetrable National Park. This is a pastime that is fast gaining popularity amongst tourists.

A pair of crested cranes take off in a magnificent flight at Lake Mburo National Park. The crane is Uganda's national bird and forms part of the court of arms. Cranes breed in wetlands after a courtship known as the "mating dance".

The rare shoebill or whale-headed stork, scientific name 'Balaeniceps rex'. This prehistoric-looking bird, with its hooked bill and baleful yellow eyes is a delight to see (if you are lucky enough to spot it in swamps). The stock is 1.5 metres tall, with a lifespan of 40 to 50 years. It is only distantly related to storks and herons. Its habitat is in the papyrus swamps and is most likely to be seen on River Nile in Murchison Falls, on the southern fringes of Lake Albert, Lake Kyoga and south of Entebbe on Lake Victoria. It is estimated that about 1000 of these birds survive in Uganda. One of them is always in the aviary at Uganda Wildlife Education Centre.

streets of Kampala, you will see the huge and rather grotesque Marabou Stork, rummaging in the rubbish dumps. Kampala's suburban gardens are a profusion of birdlife This is quite a startling sight, seeing as in other African countries, these birds are only found in the bushveld, scavenging over dead animal carcasses. Uganda also

Pink-backed pelicans and cormorants are attracted to Uganda's extensive wetlands

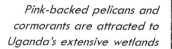

A majestic African fish eagle swoops down to grab a fish with its deadly talons on Lake Victoria. There is nothing more haunting and thrilling than the distinct far call of the fish eagle, which reminds you that you are in the heart of Africa.

Blasio Byekwaso

The pretty woodland kingfisher, easily recognised by his bright orange beak and aqua-marine blue and black wing-shoulder. This is just one of the many beautiful kingfishers found in Uganda.

The strange looking open-billed stork, is a large black waterbird whose bill has a gap when closed. Hence the appropriate name.

A brightly coloured Agama Lizard stands out with its gaudy orange, purple-navy and black scales.

A pair of mating grasshoppers blend perfectly into the background vegetation, keeping themselves well camouflaged.

A black and white spotted butterfly alights on a mauve flowering plant. This particular species is common in the yard in Kampala.

has a wonderful variety of waterbirds, savannah species and woodland birds. Wherever you go, birds are beautiful and bounteous.

Uganda is also rich in insect life and is particularly noted for its beautiful butterflies and moths. More than 144 species of butterflies have been identified in Kibale, some 300 in Semliki and over 202 in Bwindi. Some more unusual species include the huge "moon moth" and the "Congo long-tailed blue butterfly" from the western part of the country. Also abundant are ants and termites, especially in the forests. Interesting are the safari ants which move in huge swarms over long distances, and can inflict a painful bite, but are otherwise harmless. The weird-looking chameleon plays a powerful role in local superstitions. Many African Ugandans are very afraid of them, yet they

too are harmless. Also plentiful are skinks, geckos and brightly coloured lizards. Uganda has many different species of snakes, 40 percent of which are poisonous, but they tend to be shy and are seldom seen. Grasshoppers are common, as are very 'vocal' frogs that croak noisily come evening time. Insects and reptiles have to be as unobtrusive as possible to escape predators, yet at times they have to make themselves visible (or audible) to other members of the same species. This is quite a paradox, but they manage it with signals such as bright colours, or even changing colours, particular noises or strong odours. Their very survival depends on these adaptations.

An adult gorilla can grow up to 1.8 m tall and weigh up to 210 kg. There are three sub-species of gorilla found in Africa: the western lowland gorilla, the

Paul Goldring

A "Silverback" mountain gorilla bares its fangs in aggression at Bwindi Impenetrable National Park.

eastern lowland gorilla and the mountain gorilla which is the species found in Uganda and is also the most endangered. Their numbers are estimated at about 650, some in the Virunga Mountains (shared by Uganda, Congo and Rwanda), the others in Bwindi in Uganda. They are sociable animals living in troops of between 5 and 35. The male's back turns silver when he reaches sexual maturity at about 13 years old. He is the leader with a harem of three or four wives and several younger animals. The silverback may lead a troop well into his 40s. Mountain gorillas are primarily vegetarians, but also eat insects and ants for added protein. They spend most of their time on the ground but some of them move into the trees at night where each troop member builds itself a temporary nest out of leaves, branches and vines.

Chimps live in troops of between 10 and 120 animals. (Did you know that our DNA is 97.9 % the same as theirs?!) They have a definite hierarchy, headed by an alpha male. Movement between communities is not uncommon. They are terribly affectionate animals, and

Above and below: The sociable chimpanzees, also part of the ape family and more closely related to man than any other animal.

also very dramatic. Chimps are often seen "screeching" at one another, and acting very distressed for the smallest reason. Mother-child bonds are very strong and can endure sometimes for 30 or 40 years. Chimpanzees eat fruit and the tender but bitter shoots of plants which they use to make their beddings, but will occasionally eat meat, for instance other monkeys or small antelope. Chimps are extremely intelligent and in the USA they have been taught to communicate in American sign language, using over 500 words. Sadly in Africa, their numbers are dwindling due to poaching, capturing for exportation as pets, and destruction of habitat.

John Gibbons

The Red-tailed monkey is quite a widespread forest monkey. It has a distinctive brownish coat, white cheek whiskers, a red tail and a pretty heart-shaped white patch on its nose.

Ian Rheeder

Colobus monkeys in the Botanical Gardens, Entebbe. This is a beautifully-marked little animal with a distinctive black body, white facial markings that line a black face, a white side stripe and a long white tail with a shaggy tassel on the end. It is a spectacular sight watching an adult jumping up to 30 metres from tree to tree, with its white tail streaming behind.

The gentle giants — Rothchild's giraffe gather together in the savannah grasslands of Murchison Falls National Park. On the horizon, the clouds have darkened and a storm is brewing. Giraffes were re-introduced in other parks like Kidepo recently after their numbers went down.

view across the south end of Murchison Falls National Park, showing the typical semi-wooded and grassland vegetation here abundant wildlife thrives.

A topi antelope in Ishasha, (Queen Elizabeth National Park). They are often seen singly or in pairs, standing on top of a mound or anthill, which gives the topi a good vantage point, perhaps to watch out for predators.

Giant forest hogs in Queen Elizabeth National Park. They are similar in look to warthogs but are larger, with rough shaggy hair, a bushpig-type snout and smaller tusks if any.

Paul Goldring

Kirsten Durward

An african elephant standing in a swamp in the Queen Elizabeth National Park. Two races of elephants are found in Uganda: the smaller and hairy 'forest elephant' of the West African rainforest and the larger 'savannah elephant'.

A baby warthog playfully climbs over its parent's back. This is the most visible 'swine' species in Uganda. They have impressive little tusks and are comical creatures, especially when trotting away briskly in the opposite direction with their tails standing upright in the air.

Blasio Byekwaso

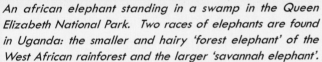

Young, free and single ... A male Uganda Kob in the grassy plains of Murchison Falls National Park. In the background are scattered Borassus palms. This animal is Uganda's national antelope and appears on the court of arms, and resembles an impala, but is much bulkier in appearance.

Blasio Byekwaso

A large buffalo feeding in the grasslands of Murchison Falls National Park. When found alone or in pairs, they can be very aggressive and dangerous. However, when part of a large herd, they generally do not pose a threat to man. In Queen Elizabeth National Park, some of the buffaloes are reddish in colour, due to interbreeding with the redder race of buffalo that lives in the Congolese rainforest.

A majestic male lion (right), called king of the African jungle. ... Park, Murchison Falls National Park and Kidepo National Park...

Paul Goldring

Eddie Kitayimbwa

Zebra stripes always paint a beautiful picture. The common or Burchell's zebra occur in Lake Mburo National Park and Kidepo National Park. They thrive in drier, savannah-type vegetation. Mature stallions gather small harems of mares, and there is a definite heiraichy evident within the herd of 10 or more.

In Uganda they are still found in Queen Elizabeth National Uganda is also known for its tree-climbing lions of Ishasha.

141

A hippo quietly surfaces in the Kazinga Channel, Queen Elizabeth National Park. It is one of the largest land animals and can weigh up to 3200 kg. Hippopotamus are strongly territorial, living in groups of 10 or more. They are quick tempered and cause more human deaths than any other herbivore in Africa, exceeding even that of big cats and crocodiles combined. (Photo: Nikki Grant)

Photo Credits

Alex Kininda Kakaine
Allan Forward
Andy Pol
Blasio Byekwaso
Brad Weltzien
Charles Maloba
Chris Billington
E. R. M. Musiime
Eddie Kitayimbwa
Edward Kamugisha
Francis Kirya
Fred Kasozi
Freddie Kasozi
Henry Bongyereirwe
Ian Rheeder

James Akena
James Sempa
Jane de Staepoole
Jane Goldring
Janet Nakimera
John Gibbons
John Mary Kabigyoma
Kirsten Durward
Kizito Malumba
Mathias Mugisha
Michael Jensen
Michael Nsubuga
Morgan Mbabazi
New Vision Library
Nikki Grant

Nuwagaba C. Tumusiime
Paul Goldring
Peter Busomoke
Richard Gampp
Robin Rheeder
Rosie Thompson
Sam Kalema
Sarah Jones
Sid Adams
Vincent Mugaba
Volker Riehl
W. W. Obote
Wilkins E. Kyawe
William Chemnoir
William Kazoora

Bibliography

Phillip Briggs, *Uganda, the Bradt Travel Guide* (3rd Edition).

Adam Seftel, *Uganda, the Bloodstained Pearl of Africa and its Struggle for Peace* (from the pages of DRUM).

Philips Rorash & Heineman, *A New Primary Social Studies Atlas for Uganda*.

Mugisha Odrek Rwabwoogo, *Uganda Districts Information Handbook*.

David Isingoma and Tom Tibaijuka, *Kampala General Handbook 1998*.

Richard Nzita and Mbaga Niwampa, *Peoples and Cultures of Uganda*.

David Mukholi, *Uganda's Fourth Constitution*.

Camerapix, *Spectrum Guide to UGANDA*.

Airlines

Africaone

Plot 13-15 Kimathi Avenue
P.O. Box 2128
Tel: + 256 41 344520/346980
+ 256 31 261212/261213
Website: www.flyafricaone.com

Air India Ltd.,

Plot 6/6A, Nile Avenue
Grand Imperial Hotel
Shopping Arcade
Tel: 320677, 342655,
230600
Fax: 250605

Air Tanzania Corporation

Plot 1, Kimathi Avenue
Tel: 234673, 234631
Fax: 234673

British Airways

Ternan Avenue
Tel: 257414/6
(reservations)
234907 (executive club)
256695 (administration)
Fax: 259181
Website: www.britishways.com

Dairo Air Services

Plot 24, Jinja Road
Tel: 257731, 344242
Fax: 259242
Telex: 61487

Eagle Air

Plot 11 Adam House,
Portal Avenue,
Tel: 344292
Fax: 344501
Entebbe Airport: 320601
320782, 320516
e-mail: eagle@swiftuganda.com
website: www.eagleuganda.com

Egyptair

Nile Avenue,
Grand Imperial Shopping
Arcade
Tel: 341276, 233960
Fax: 236567
E-mail : Egyptairuganda@microskillsug.com

Emirates Airlines

Kimathi Avenue
(Former Neeta Cinema)
Tel: 349941/4
Fax: 340076
Mob: 075 690685

Ethiopian Airlines

Plot 1, Kimathi Avenue
United Assurance Blg,
Tel: 345118, 345577/8
Fax: 231455
e-mail: klaetam@swiftuganda.com
website: www. flyethiopia. com

Gulf Air

Plot 1, Kimathi Avenue
United Assurance Building
Tel: 343190, 343105,
230526, 230524
Fax: 343210

Kenya Airways

United Assurance Big,
Kimathi Avenue
Tel: 344304, 233068,
256506
Fax: 259472
Satelite phone: 870 762557510
e-mail: kenyaair@swiftuganda. com

Mission Aviation Fellowship (MAF)

Plot 260/255, Kizungu
Lane, Makindye,
Tel: 268388, 267462
Fax: 267433
e-mail: maf. uganda@maf. org

South African Airways

Ground Floor, Workers'
House
Plot 1, Pilkington Road
Tel: 345772/3/5, 25501,
Fax: 345774
e-mail: saa@kla. flysaa. com

United Airlines (U) Ltd.,

Pan African House,
Kimathi Avenue
Tel: 349841/2, 320516/9
(Entebbe Airport)
Fax: 3221779

Reliance Air (U) Ltd.

Entebbe Airport,
Tel: 321251/5
Fax: 321343
E-mail: reliance@airserve. org
Website: http: www. airserve.org

Apartments

Blacklines House, Kampala

P. O. Box 6968
Plot 2, Colville Street
Phone: 256-41-342913
Alt. Phone: 256-41-236441
Fax: 256-41-255288

Elite Apartments, Kampala

41/A/B Nkrumah Road
Phone: 256-41-341877
Alt. Phone: 256-41-798765
Fax: 256-41-349968

Golf Course Apartments, Kampala

P. O. Box 22774
Plot 5, Makindu Close
Phone: 256-41-342745
Alt. Phone: 256-41-342769
Fax: 256-41-235674

Mosa Court Apartments, Kampala

P. O. Box 2186
Plot 12, Shimoni Rd
Phone: 256-41-230321
Alt. Phone: 256-41-230292
Fax: 256-41-230310

Salama Springs, Kampala

Plot 76, Old Port Bell Rd, Bugolobi
Phone: 256-41-223027*
Alt. Phone: 256-41-223026
Fax: 256-41-223028

Spear House Ltd, Kampala

P. O. Box 10
Plot 22, Jinja Rd, Spear House
Phone: 256-41-234903
Alt. Phone: 256-41-259856
Fax: 256-41-235658

Speke Apartments, Kampala

P. O. Box 7036
Plot 7/9 Wampewo Ave
Phone: 256-41-346174
Alt. Phone: 256-41-346175
Fax: 256-41-235345

Banks

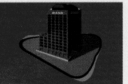

Allied Bank International (U) Ltd, Jinja

P. O. Box 2095
Plot 1, Main Street
Phone 256-41-1212

Allied Bank International (U) Ltd., Kampala

P. O . Box 2750
Plot 24 Jinja Rd
Phone 256-41-236535
Alt. Phone 256-41-236536
Fax 256-41-230439

Bank of Uganda, Kampala

P. O. Box 7120
Plot 37/43 Kampala Rd.
Tel: 256 41 258441/6
258090, 232396, 258060/9
Fax: 256 41 233818, 230978

Barclays Bank, Kampala

P. O. Box 2971
Plot 16, Kampala Rd
Phone 256-41-233998
Fax 256-41-230146

Cairo International Bank Ltd, Kampala

P. O. Box 7052
Phone 256-41-230141
Alt. Phone 256-41-230136
Fax 256-41-230135

Centenary Rural Development Bank Ltd., Kampala

P. O. Box 19892
Plot 7, Entebbe Rd, Talenta House
Phone 256-41-251276
Alt. Phone 256-41-251277
Fax 256-41-232393

CitiBank Uganda Limited, Kampala

P. O. Box 7505
Plot 4 Terman Avenue Nakasero
Phone 256-41-
Alt. Phone 256-41-
Fax 256-41-

Crane Bank Ltd, Kampala

P. O. Box 22572
Plot 38, Kampala Rd, Crane Chambers
Phone 256-41-345345
Alt. Phone 256-41-341414
Fax 256-41-231578

EADB Bank, Kampala

P. O. Box 7128
Plot 4, Nile Ave.
Phone 256-41-230021
Fax 256-41-259763

Equator Bank PLC (HSBC), Kampala

P. O. Box 1251
Plot 1, Lumumba Ave.
Rwenzori House
Phone 256-41-250696
Alt. Phone 256-41-250538

National Bank of Commerce (U) Ltd. Kampala

P. O. Box 23232
Plot 13, Parliament Ave.
Cargen House
Phone 256-41-347700
Alt. Phone 256-41-347702
Fax 256-41-347701

Nile Bank Ltd, Kampala

P. O Box 2834
Plot 22, Jinja, Rd, Spear House

Banks Cont...

Orient Bank, Kampala

P. O. Box 3072
Plot 10, Kampala Rd,
Uganda House
Phone: 256-41-236012
Alt. Phone: 256-41-236013
Fax: 256-41-236066
P. O. Box 7197
Plot 18, Kampala Rd
Phone: 256-41-232783
Alt. Phone: 256-41-236192
Fax: 256-41-258263

Post Bank Ltd. Kampala

P. O. Box 7189
Plot 68-70, William Street,
Post Bank House
Phone: 256-41-343932
Alt. Phone: 256-41-258619
Fax: 256-41-347107

Stanbic Bank, Kampala

P. O. Box 7131
Tel: +256 41 231151, 231152
Fax: +256 41 231116

Standard Chartered Bank, Kampala

P. O. Box 7111
Plot 5, Speke Rd,
Standard Chartered Bank
Building
Phone: 256-41-258211
Alt. Phone: 256-41-258217
Fax: 256-41-231473

Tropical Africa Bank Ltd. Kampala

P. O. Box 9485
Plot 27, Kampala Rd
Phone: 256-41-231990
Alt. Phone: 256-41-231993
Fax: 256-41-232297

U, P&Temly. Co. op Saving & Credit Society Ltd, Kampala

P. O. Box 1031
Kampala Rd. G. P. O
Building
Phone: 256-41-348470
Alt. Phone: 256-41-257406

Uganda Commercial Bank, Kampala

P. O. Box 7073
Plot 12, Kampala Rd., City
Branch
Phone: 256-41-341155
Alt. Phone: 256-41-255527

Uganda Commercial Bank, Kampala

P. O. Box 973
Plot 12, Kampala Rd,
Phone: 256-41-234710
Alt. Phone: 256-41-234723
Fax: 256-41-259012

World Bank, Kampala

P. O. Box 4463
Plot 1 Lumumba Ave.
Rwenzori House
Phone: 256-41-230094
Alt. Phone: 256-41-231061
Fax: 256-41-230092

Bars & Restaurants

Al's Bar

Ggaba Road, Kansanga

Andy the Greek's

Plot 30, Windsor Crescent
Tel: 077 405578

Capital Pub

Plot 7, Ggaba Road,
Kabalagala
Tel: 269676

City Bar

Plot 11, Kampala Road
Tel: 346460

Cooper Road Bistro & Bar

Plot 7, Copper Road
Tel: 235134
Fax: 231652

Crocodile

Plot 21, Kisementi
Tel: 254593

DV8 Bar and Bistro

Plot 10, Wilson Road
(Cineplex Blg)
Tel: 347713, 348055

Half London

Plot 70, Ggaba Road
Tel: 268910

Jokers Sports

Plot 109 Buganda Road
Tel: 348417
e-mail: jokers@starcom.
co. ug

Just Kicking

Plot 5, Cooper Road,
Kisementi
Kamwokya
Tel: 235134
Fax: 231652

Kaos Sports Bar,

Kitante Road,
Tel: 250371, 075 786678
Fax: 343533
E-mail: havana@starcom.
co. ug

Korner Café, Gulu

Coronation Road, Plot 1
Tel: 077-453190

La Bella Bar

Plot 1, Dewinton Road
Tel: 236123

La Fontaine

Plot 6, Bukoto Street
Tel: 077 406197
Africa Village
Buganda Road
Mob: 075 643115, 077
483813

On the Rocks

Speke Hotel, Nile Avenue

Pub Mamma Mia

Speke Hotel

Rhino Bar

Ternan Avenue, Sheraton
Hotel

Slow Boat

Plot 2, Kampala Road
Tel: 255647

Car Hire

ABM Taxi Services, Kampala

P. O Box 21332,
Ternan Avenue, Sheraton Hotel
Phone: 256-41-344590

Afrique Voyages Ltd, Kampala

P. O Box 10805,
Plot 3, Parliament Avenue, Raja Chambers
Phone: 256-41-230336
Alt. Phone: 256-41-251366
Fax: 256-41-342437

Avis Rent a Car, Entebbe

Arrival Hall, Entebbe
Phone: 256-41-320516
Alt. Phone: 256-41-320518

Avis Rent a Car, Kampala

P. O Box 11970,
Plot 1, Kimathi Avenue, Airlines Building
Phone: 256-41-254521
Fax: 256-41-257278

B&B Car Hire & Sales, Kampala

P. O Box 222,
Plot 32, Nile Avenue, Inter. Conf. Centre Rm 164
Phone: 256-41-346926
Fax: 256-41-346296

Belex Taxis, Kampala

Sheraton Hotel, Ternan Avenue
Phone: 256-41-344105
Alt. phone: 256-41344590

Belex Tours & Travel Ltd, Kampala

P. O Box 10542,
Plot 4, Ternan Avenue, Sheraton Avenue
Phone: 256-41-344590
Alt. Phone: 256-41-234180
Fax: 256-41234252

C & A Tours & Travel Operators, Entebbe

Entebbe
Phone: 256-41-320516

C&A Tours & Travel Operators Ltd, Kampala

P. O Box 23456,
Plot 1, Colville Street
Phone: 256-41-347191
Alt. Phone: 256-41-347192
Fax: 256-41-347192

Car Marts

Lonrho Motors Uganda Ltd, Kampala
P. O Box 353,
45 Jinja Road
Phone: +256-41-340890/4
Alt. Phone: +256-41-231395, 340894
Fax: +256-41-254388

Cars Ltd, Kampala

P. O Box 9006,
Plot 4, Lumum Street
Phone: 256-41-256656

City Cars Ltd, Kampala

P. O Box 151,
Muyenga Rd, Tank Hill Parade, First Flr. Rm. 20
Phone: 256-41-268611
Fax: 256-41-232338

Expart Crankshaft Regrinders Ltd, Kampala

P. O Box 24309 Kampala,
Plot 394 Kagugude, Kampala
Phone: 256-41-230371
Alt. Phone: 256-41-230371

Flyway Ltd, Kampala

P. O Box 6236,
Plot 40, Kampala Rd
Phone: 256-41-254654
Alt. Phone: 256-41-257208

Car Parks

Green Boat Entertainment Ltd, Kampala

P. O Box 23027,
Plot 32, Nakasero Rd
Phone: 256-41-251229
Alt. Phone: 256-41-232350
Fax: 256-41-345562
Global Hire Services, Jinja
P. O Box 11970,
Plot 6A, Clive Rd
Phone: 256-43-120110
Fax: 256-43-120110

Hertz Rent a Car, Entebbe

P. O Box 24,
Phone: 256-41-320516

Hertz, Kampala

Communications House (Ground Floor) Colville street
Phone: 256-77-450460
Alt. Phone: 256-77-408713

Kings Autocentre Ltd, Kampala

P. O Box 12848,
726 Gaba Road-Kabalagala
Phone: 256-41-268009
Alt. Phone: 256-41-269200
Fax: 256-41-251751

New Lines, Kampala

Fairway Hotel, Kampala
Phone: 256-41-251752
Alt. Phone: 256-75-721111

Nile Safaris, Kampala

P. O Box 12135,
Plot 8/10, Kampala Rd,
Uganda House Shop 3
Phone: 256-41-258603
Alt. Phone: 256-41-345092
Fax: 256-41-345092

Nis Uganda, Kampala

P. O Box 12704 Kampala,
Plot 95 Jinja Road
Phone: 256-41-251755
Alt. Phone: 256-41-234977
Fax: 256-41-251751

Phoenix Car Hire & Tours, Kampala

P. O Box 3127,
Rwenzori House, 1
Lumumba Avenue
Phone: 256-41-236096
Alt. Phone: 256-77-200605
Fax: 256-41-236998

Rhino Car Rentals, Kampala

P. O Box 23456,
Plot 1, Colville Street
Phone: 256-41-234295
Fax: 256-41-344636

Safaris Expeditions Ltd, Kampala

P. O Box 6686,
Plot 56/60, Kampala Rd,
Ambassodor House
Phone: 256-41-255943
Fax: 256-41-255944

Skill Car Rental, Kampala

P. O Box 12795,
Hotel Equatorial
Phone: 256-41-250780
Alt. Phone: 256-77-408713

Spear Motors Ltd, Kampala

P. O Box 1350, Kampala,
Nakawa
Phone: 256-41-222696/7/8
Alt. Phone: 256-41-231380

Swiftlink Tours & Travel Ltd, Kampala

P. O Box 7057,
Nile Avenue
Phone: 256-41-258081
Alt. Phone: 256-41-258088
Fax: 256-41-234316

The Travel Group, Kampala

P. O Box 7743, Kampala
Cooper Road, Plot 1
Phone: 256-41-345979:
Fax: 256-41-345979

Clinics & Hospitals

Abii Clinic & Laboratory Services, Kampala

P. O Box 10281,
Bombo Road, Wandegeya
Phone: 256-41-543-602

Agape Nursing Home, Kiboga

P. O Box 190,
Buzibweera Road
Phone: 256-465-2329
Alt. Phone: 256-465-2360

Andrew Medical Centre, Kampala

P. O Box 11257,
Plot 1, Bombo Road , Sure House
Phone: 256-41-232-668
Alt. Phone: 256-75-693-465
Fax: 256-41-232-668

Bunawona Clinic, Jinja

P. O Box 131,
Plot 7A, Nizam Road East
Phone: 256-77-463-029

Busingye Medical Centre, Kampala

P. O Box 16004,
Plot 3/5, Bombo Road
Phone: 256-41-259-814

Byansi Clinic, Masaka

P. O Box 1461,
Plot 9, Kampala Road
Phone: 256-481-21433
Fax: 256-481-20388

C. K Mugabe, Kabarole

P. O Box408,
Plot 1, Balya Road, Fort Portal
Phone: 256-483-22638

Case Clinic, Kampala

P. O Box 4547,
Buganda Road, next to Roots Club,
Phone: 256-41-250-362
Alt. Phone: 256-75-750-362
Fax: 256-41-286-626

Clive Road Clinic, Jinja

P. O Box 880,
Plot 12C, Clive Road
Phone: 256-43-120-149

Dr. Ganaga E. J Medical Clinic, Kasese

P. O Box 153,
Plot 14, Margherita Street
Phone: 256-483-44304

Dr. J. B Ntege's Clinic, Kampala

Ug. Teachers' Association Building,
Plot 28/30, Bombo Road
Phone: 256-41-254-185

Egof Medical Centre, Jinja

P. O Box 660,
Plot 5, Owen Road
Phone: 256-43-122-125

EMCo Medical & Hearing Centre, Kampala

P. O Box 1552,
Plot 10, Kampala Road,
Uganda House
Phone: 256-41-250-673
Alt. Phone: 256-77-495-650

Entebbe Central Clinic, Entebbe

P. O Box 54, Entebbe
Phone: 256-41-320-893

Gulu Family Clinic, Gulu

P. O Box 703,
Plot 2, Coronation Road,
Harambee Building
Phone: 256-900-179

Hoima Islamic Health Centre, Hoima

P. O Box202,
Fort Portal Road
Phone: 256-456-40143

Industrial Medical Services, Kampala

P. O Box 11538,
Plot 18, Jinja Road,
Madhvani Building
Phone: 256-41-254-554
Alt. Phone: 256-41-256-347

International Medical Centre, Kampala

P. O Box 22803,
Plot 87, Kampala Road, K
P C Building,
Also Kitgum House, Jinja Road
Phone: 256-41-341-291
Alt. Phone: 256-41-342-608
Fax: 256-41-342-608

Jinja Medical Centre, Jinja

P. O Box 43,
Plot 88/89, Main Street
Phone: 256-43-122-260
Alt. Phone: 256-43-121-446

Kabale Surgery Clinic, Kabale

P. O Box 1102,
Plot 58, Kabale Road
Phone: 256-486-24384
Alt. Phone: 256-486-24297

Kadic Medical Consultants, Kampala

Makerere Hill Road,
Plot, 763
Phone: 256-41-530-046
Fax: 256-41-530-412

Kampala Medical Chambers Clinic, Kampala

P. O Box 3479,
Plot 14A, Buganda Road
Phone: 256-41-348-846

Marie Stopes Clinic, Kampala

P. O Box 10431,
Plot 286, Makerere Kavule
Phone: 256-41-531-255

Mayanja Mememorial Nursing Home, Mbarara

P. O Box 920,
Plot 44, Bucunku Lane
Phone: 256-485-21825
Alt. Phone: 256-485-21116

Mayo Clinic, Kampala

P. O Box2591,
Plot 40, NITCO Building,
Bombo Road
Phone: 256-41-250-623
Alt. Phone: 256-77-403-760
Fax: 256-41-250-623

Mbale Parent's Clinic & Laboratory, Mbale

P. O Box 516,
Plot 20/22, Republic Street
Phone: 256-45-33787

Naguru Medical Laboratory, Kampala

P. O Box 4295,
Plot 2, Sports Lane
Phone: 256-41-222-715
Fax: 256-41-222-715

Next Clinic & Laboratory Services, Lira

P. O Box 281,
Plot 44, Lira Avenue, Next
Building
Phone: 256-473-20281
Alt. Phone: 256-473-20234
Fax: 256-473-20588

Nyondo Clinic, Kampala

P. O Box 8217, Plot 13B,
Kampala Road, Opp.
Crown House
Phone: 256-41-258-738
Alt. Phone: 256-77-435-680
Fax: 256-41-234248

Public Drug Store, Arua

P. O Box 306,
Plot 16, Avenue Road
Phone: 256-476-20320

St. Anthony's Clinic, Lugazi

P. O Box 112, Plot 18A
Ntenga Road
Phone: 256-41-48287

St. Catherine's Clinic, Kampala

P. O Box 3760,
Plot 50, Kampala Road
Phone: 256-41-231-534
Alt. Phone: 256-77-430-628

Theta, Kampala

P. O Box 21175,
Plot 723, Mawanda Road,
Kamwokya
Phone: 256-41-530-619
Alt. Phone: 256-41-532-930
Fax: 256-41-530-619

Uhuru Clinic, Arua

P. O Box 393,
Plot 21, Duka Road
Phone: 256-476-20097

Victoria Medical Centre, Entebbe

P. O Box 723,
Plot 22, Gowers Road
Phone: 256-41-320-956

X-Ray Clinic, Kampala

P. O Box 1006,
Plot 43, Nkurumah Road,
Pan World Centre
Phone: 256-41-345-095
Fax: 256-41-345-095

Couriers

Daks Couriers (UPS) Ltd, Kampala

P. O Box 487,
Crown House, Plot 4,
Kampala Road
Phone: +256-41-340405
Fax: +256-41-234843

DHL International (U) Ltd, Kampala

P. O Box 1623,
Plot 2, Colville Street,
Blacklines House
Phone: 256-41-256470
Alt. Phone: 256-41-256345
Fax: 256-41-256236

Elma Express Delivery Ltd, Kampala

P. O Box 2260,
Plot 29/33 K'la Rd, Amber House
Phone: 256-41-257364
Fax: 256-41-257364

Federal Express (FedEx), Kampala

P. O Box 353,
Entebbe Rd, Metropole House
Phone: 256-41-347918
Alt. Phone: 256-41-231168
Fax: 256-41-347917

Skynet Worldwide Express, Kampala

P. O Box 4246,
Plot 16, Old Port Bell Road,
Industrial Area, Skynet House
Phone: 256-41-235-269
Alt. Phone: 256-41-236-393
Fax: 256-41-343-380

TNT Express Worldwide, Kampala

P. O Box 6449,
Shimoni Rd, Nile International, Conference Centre
Phone: 256-41-230005
Alt. Phone: 256-41-236154
Fax: 256-41-255385

TransAfrica Air Express Couriers Ltd, Kampala

P. O Box 2393,
Plot 2, Colville Street,
Blacklines House
Phone: 256-41-255267
Alt. Phone: 256-41-255200
Fax: 256-41-255267

Uganda Post Ltd, Kampala

P. O Box 7106,
Plot 35, Kampala Rd
Phone: 256-41-256151
Fax: 256-41-232564

Yellow pages Express Mail Service Ltd, Mbarara

P. O Box 1199,
Plot 45A, High Street
Phone: 256-485-20430

Dental

Begumanya Dental Care Centre, Mbarara

P. O Box 398,
Plot 4, Buremba Rd

Dental Public Health Mulago, Kampala

P. O Box 10562,
Phone: 256-41-540439
Alt. Phone: 256-41-554001
Fax: 256-41-530412

Dr. G. W. Ssamula's Dental Clinic, Kampala

P. O Box 960,
Plot 8/19, Nkrumah Rd,
Uganda House
Phone: 256-41-258338
Alt. Phone: 256-41-258332

Dr. Ntwatwa S. Lule Dental Clinic, Kampala

P. O Box 25523,
Plot 220, Hoima Rd
Phone: 256-41-250312

Dr. P. O Aliker Dental Surgeon, Kampala

P. O Box 249,
Plot 50, Lumumba Ave
Phone: 256-41-254858
Fax: 256-41-254858

Jubilee Dental, Kampalaa

P. O Box 23015,
Plot 18B, Buganda Rd
Phone: 256-41-344647

Kisekka Dental Clinic, Kampala

P. O Box 8727,
Plot 40, Bombo Rd
Phone: 256-41-250312

Madan's Dental Centre, Kampala

P. O Box 16121,
Plot 65, Kiira Rd, Kamwokya
Phone: 256-41-543058
Alt. Phone: 256-41-349284

Pan Denatal Surgery, Kampala

P. O Box 11995,
Plot 45, Nkurumah Rd,
Musana House
Phone: 256-41-251525
Alt. Phone: 256-41-347608
Fax: 256-41-251525

St. Jude Dental Wing (Mbarara Nursing Home), Mbarara

P. O Box 1626,
Plot 11, Makhan Singh Street, Mbarara Nursing Home
Phone: 256-485-20174
Alt. Phone: 256-485-20959
Fax: 256-485-20782

Tekk Densaid Plus, Kampala

P. O Box 7062,
Plot 241, Makerere Hill Rd.

Uganda Dental Supplies Ltd, Kampala

P. O Box 151,
Parliament Ave, Baumann House
Phone: 256-41-232335
Alt. Phone: 256-41-232328

Game Lodges

Arra Fishing Lodge, Adjumani

P. O Box Adjumani
Phone: +256-41-342926
Fax: +256-41-342995

Bulago Island, kalangala

P. O Box Bulago,
Phone: +256-77-709970

Bushara Island Camp, Lake Bunyonyi, Kabale

Bushara Island,
Phone: +256-486-23743
Fax: +256-486-23742

Crater Valley Kibale (CVK) Forest Resort, Fort Portal

13km on Fort-Portal Kamwenge Road
Phone: 256-41-492274
Fax: 256-483-22636

Far Out Camp, Lake Bunyonyi, Kabale

Phone: +256-486-22175, 075-702233
Alt. Phone: (+256)77-409510, 41-235494, 75
Fax: +256-486-23742

Gately On Nile, Jinja

34B Nile Crescent, Jinja
Phone: +256-43-122400
Alt. Phone: +256-77-469638
E-mail: gately@source. co.ug

Islands Club, Ssese Islands, Kalangala

Buggala Island,
Phone: +256-41-231386
Alt. Phone: +256-77-504027, 501574
Fax: +256-41-231385

Jacana Safari Lodge, Queen Elizabeth National Park, Kampala

Jacana Safari Lodge,
Phone: +256-41-258273
Fax: +256-41-233992

Mantana Luxury Tented Camps,

Lake Mburo, Mbarara
Phone: +256-41-3201152
Alt. Phone: (+256)41-321552, 77-401391

Mweya safari Lodge, Queen Elizabeth National park, Kampala

P. O Box 22827 Kampala,
Phone: +256-78-260260/1
Alt. Phone: +256-77-788887
Fax: +256-78-260262

Ndali Lodge, Crater Lakes, Fort Portal

Phone: +256-483-22636
Fax: +256-483-22636

Nile River Explorers Backpackers Camp, Jinja

41 Wilson Road
Phone: 256-43-1202236
Alt. Phone: 256-77-422373
Fax: 256-43-121322

Nile Safari Camp, Murchison Falls National Park, Masindi

Inns of Uganda,
Phone: +256-41-258273
Fax: +256-41-233992

Paraa Safari Lodge, Muchison Falls National Park, Masindi

Phone: +256-78-260260
Alt. Phone: +256-77-788887
Fax: +256-78-260262

Rwenzori View Guest House, Fort portal

15 Lower Kakiza Road, Fort Portal,
15 Lower Kakiza Road, Boma
Phone: +256-483-22102
Alt. Phone: +256-77722102

Sambiya River Lodge

Murchison Falls National park
Bking; Afritours &Travel Ltd
Phone 041-344855

Samuka Island, Jinja

Phone: +256-43-121301
Alt. Phone: +256-77-401508/9
Fax: +256-43-121301

Semliki Safari Lodge, Bundibugyo,

Phone: +256-77-709970

Volcanoes Tented Camps @ Sipi, Bwindi & Mgahinga

P. O Box 22818 Kampala,
27 Lumumba Avenue,
Nakasero Hill, Kampala
Phone: +256-41-346464
Alt. Phone: +256-75-741718
Fax: +256-41-341718
E-mail: Sales@volcanoes safaris. Com

Hotels & Motels

AB Top End Guest House, Lira

P. O. Box 446
Plot 80 Oyam Road

ABC Hotel, Kampala

P. O. Box 9211
Plot 35 Nakivubo Place, Ziba Building
Phone 256-41-340100

Acholi Inn Hotel

P. O. Box 239
Plot 4/6, Elizabeth Rd
Phone 256-900-108

Agip Motel-Mbarara-Mbarara

P. O. Box 1191
Masaka Road
Phone 256-0485-21615

Alaba Paradise Inn, Malaba

P. O. Box 42
Morukasipe Road
Phone 256-045-42012

Andrews Inn, Mbarara

P. O. Box 1310
Plot 47 Moti Kakiika Street
Phone 256-0485-20247

Annes Worth Guest House, Jinja

P. O. Box 1253
Plot 3 Nalugenya Road
Phone 256-43-12006

Athina Club House, Kampala

P. O. Box 8717
Plot 30, Winsor Crescent, Kololo
Phone: 256-41-341428
Fax: 256-41-236089

Backpackers Hostel & Campsite,

Lungujja, Kampala
P. O. Box 6121, Kampala
Kalema Road
Phone: +256-41-344417
Alt. Phone: +256-77-430587

Banda Island Resort, Kampala

P. O. Box 6968
Plot 1, Banda Island
Phone: 256-41-255267
Fax: 256-41-255288

Blue Cat (1996), Jinja

P. O. Box 617
Plot 4 Clive Road
Phone 256-43-122137

Botanical Garden Guest House, Mbale

P. O. Box 484
Bungoko Senior Quarters
Phone: 256-045-33185
Alt. Phone: 256-045-34068

Broadway Cultural Centre & Guest House, Entebbe

P. O. Box 315
Entebbe Road
Phone 256041-320887

Bwayo Guest Centre, Luweero

P. O. Box 333, Luweero
Tandekwire Road
Phone 941-610188

Campus Castella Motel, Kampala

P. O. Box 60274
Bombo Rd
Phone: 256-41-620087

Chez Johnson Hotels, Kampala

P. O. Box 30896
Bombo Rd-Kazo
Phone 256-41-542288

City view Hotel, Kampala

P. O. Box 21452
Plot 118, Mufunya Rd, Mengo
Phone 256-41-251345/6/6/7

College Inn Hotel, Kampala

P. O. Box 2980
Plot 359 Bombo Rod
Phone 256-41-533-835

Colline Hotel Ltd., Mukono

Plot 24/29 Sekibobo Road
Phone: 256-41-290-533/256-402
Alt. Phone: 256-41-290-240
Fax: 256-41-290-533

Continental Hotel, Fort Portal

P. O. Box 244
Plot 3 Lugard Rd
Phone: 256-483-22967
Alt. Phone: 256-483-22450

Crane Guest House, Entebbe

P. O. Box 33
Plot 19 Hamu Mukasa Road
Phone 256-41-320651

Crested Crane Hotel, Jinja

P. O. Box 444
Hannington Square
Phone: 256-41-121513
Alt. Phone: 256-41-121514
Fax: 256-41-121515

Crystal Hotel, Tororo

P. O. Box 778
Plot 22 Bazaar Street
Phone 256-045-44081

Daniel Hotel Ltd. Jinja

P. O. Box 1213
Plot 18D Kiira Road
Phone: 256-41-120989
Alt. Phone: 256-41-130128
Fax: 256-41-121322

Deluxe Guest House, Tororo

P. O. Tororo
10 Market Street
Phone 256-45-44986

Deluxe View Motel, Kampala

P. O. Box 40164
Phone 256-41-267372

Dolphin Suites, Kampala

P. O. Box 3927
Plot 36, Princess Anne Drive, Bugolobi
Phone: +256-41-223756
Alt. Phone: +256-41-223759
Fax: +256-41-223760

East View Guest House, Iganga

P. O. Box 446
Plot 77 Old Market Street
Phone 256-43-2172

Elly's Motel, Kampala

P. O. Mukono
Seeta Trading Centre
Phone: 256-41-290638
Alt. Phone: 256-41-290025

Ellys Motel, Mukono

P. O. Box 94
Jinja Road, Seeta
Phone: 256-41-290025
Fax: 256-41-230727

Entebbe Freight Motel, Entebbe

P. O. Box 259
Plot 20 Queens Road
Phone: 256-41-320812
Fax: 256-41-320241

Entebbe Resort Beach Ltd., Entebbe

P. O. Box 380
Mpigi Road
Phone: 256-41-320934
Alt. Phone: 256-41-320941
Fax: 256-41-32-1028

Entry View Restaurant Mbarara

P. O. Box 1252
Plot 69/71 Makhan Singh Street

Executive End Hotel Ltd Kampala

P. O. Box 5402
Masaka Rd, Busega
Phone 256-41-256332

Exotic Inn Ltd. Kampala

P. O. Box 10430
Rubaga Rd.
Phone: 256-41-271181
Alt. Phone: 256-41-533483

Fountaine, Kampala

P. O. Box 11243
Plot 6, Bukoto Street
Phone: +256-41-342100
Alt. Phone: +256-75-754979

Friends Corner Hotel Mbarara

P. O. Box 788
Bulemba Road
Phone 256-0485-21322

Frointier Club Hotel Ltd Tororo

P. O. Box 1119
Plot 12 Jowtt
Phone: 256-045-44474

Garden Inn Hotel, Lira

P. O. Box 325, Lira
Phone 256-473-20134

Gately Online Ltd. Jinja

P. O. Box 1300
Plot 3 Kisinja Road
Phone 256-43-122400

GB Rest House Muyenga Kampala

P. O. Box 1457
Plot 3304, Kironde Rd
Phone 256-41-268809

Grand Pearl Hotel Kampala

P. O. Box 9153
Plot 1230/1231, Tank Hill Rd
Phone: 256-41-267910
Fax: 256-41-267910

Grand Plaza Hotel Ltd. Kampala

P. O. Box 9211
Plot 6/6a, Shimoni Road
Phone 256-41-256093/4

Havana Ltd. Hotel Kampala

P. O. Box 2251
Plot 28, Mackaya Rd
(Opp. New Taxi Park)
Phone: 256-41-343532
Alt. Phone: 256-41-250762
Fax: 256-41-250762

Highland Hotel, Kabale

Phone 256-486-22175

Hill View Hotel, Mbale

P. O. Box 1713
Tororo Road
Phone 256-045-33075

Hills Inn Kabale, Kabale

P. O. Box 714
Plot 18 Ngorogoza Road
Phone: 256-486-24442
Alt. Phone: 256-41-486-24443

Hilltop Hotel, Kampala

P. O. Box 2783
Plot 49, Namirembe Rd.
Bakuli
Phone 256-41-270924

Homeland's Hotel, Kampala

P. O. Box 1966
Masaka Rd, Ndeeba
Phone: 256-41-272456
Fax: 256-41-272466

Hot Spot International Hotel Ltd., Busia

P. O Box 372
Plot 4 Custom Rd
Phone: 256-45-43037
Alt. Phone: 256-45-43163
Fax: 256-45-43163

Hot Springs Hotel Ltd, Bushenyi

P. O. Box 168
Plot 67, Fort Portal Rd-Ishaka
Phone 256-485-42634

Hotel Afripa Masaka

P. O. Box 1230
Plot 2 Hobert Street
Phone 256-481-201443

Hotel Aribas, Masindi

P. O. Box 56
Plot 82 Masindi Port Road
Phone 256-465-20411

Hotel Atlanta, Kayunga

P. O. Box 18281
Ssekanja Road.

Hotel Brovad Ltd., Masaka

P. O. Box 566
Plot 6 Cercular Road
Phone: 256-481-21455
Alt. Phone: 256-481-21826
Fax: 256-481-20997

Hotel Calender, Kampala

P. O Box 3796
Plot 11, Namasoole Rd (Off Mobutu Rd, Makidye)
Phone: 256-41-268557
Fax: 256-41-268557

Hotel City Square, Kampala

P. O. Box 2246
Opp. City Square, Kampala Rd.
Phone: 256-41-256257
Alt. Phone: 256-41-251451
Fax: 256-41-251440

Hotel City Way, Kampala

Plot 118, Mufunya Rd,
Mengo Rubaga
Phone: 256-41-347878

Hotel Classic Ltd, Mbarara

P. O. Box 1152
Plot 57 High Street
Phone: 256-41-20609
Fax: 256-41-20609

Hotel Dewinton, Kampala

P. O. Box 21985
Plot 36 Namirembe Rd
Phone 256-41-347846

Hotel Gloria, Tororo

P. O. Box 229
Plot 50 Jinja Road
Phone 256-045-44159

Hotel GoCool Ltd., Kampala

P. O. Box 7454
Plot 58, Nakivubo Rd
Phone 256-41-230268

Hotel Havana, Kampala

28 Mackay Road
Phone: 256-41-250762
Alt. Phone: 256-41-343532
Fax: 256-41-343533

Hotel Holiday, Kampala

P. O. Box 7883
Wakaliga Rd
Phone 256-41-272562

Hotel International, Kampala

P. O. Box 3047
Tank Hill muyenga
Phone: 256-41-266924
Alt. Phone: 256-41-266967
Fax: 256-41-269616

Hotel La Nova, Masaka

Plot 12 Hobert Street
Phone 256-481-21520

Hotel Mansy, Kampala

P. O. Box 4549
Entebbe Rd Kinuye-Kavule
Phone: 256-41-26737
Alt. Phone: 256-41-268817
Fax: 256-41-268530

Hotel Margherita Ltd., Kasese

Phone: 256-483-44015
Alt. Phone: 256-486-232183

Hotel Metropole, Kampala

P. O. Box 7602
Plot 37/38, Nakivubo Rd
Phone 256-41-235484

Hotel Millennium, Kampala

P. O. Box 11442
Zana-Entebbe Rd
Phone: 256-41-233372
Alt. Phone: 256-41-272908
Fax: 256-41-236075

Hotel Olympia, Kampala

P. O. Box 5637
Kansaga-Ggaba Rd.
Phone 256-41-266743

Hotel Regency, Kampala

P. O. Box 5545
Plot 78/79, Namirembe Rd,
Bakuli
Phone: 256-41-272337
Alt. Phone: 256-41-272338
Fax: 256-41-230490

Hotel River Side Ltd., Rukungiri

P. O. Box 225
Plot 241 Nyakibale Road
Phone 256-486-424550

Hotel Roma, Gulu

P. O. Bpx 779
Plot 16, Coronation Rd
Phone 256-900-224

Hotel Royale, Kampala

P. O. BOX 21620
Ggaba Rd Bunga
Phone 256-41-266034

Hotel Shubham, Kampala

Plot 6 Old Fort Rd, Bakuli
Phone 256-041-231367

Hotel Soka, Fort Portal

Kichwamba Trading Centre
Phone 256-483-22238

Hotel SunCity, Kampala

P. O. Box 8195
Plot 46, William Street
Phone 256-41-345542

Hotel Triangle Ltd, Jinja

P. O. Box 443
Plot 49 Fort Portal Road

Inns of Uganda, Kampala

P. O. Box 2288
Kimathi Ave, Impala House
Phone: 256-41-258273
Fax: 256-41-233992

Jeliza Hotel Co. Ltd., Kampala

P. O. Box 2800
Plot 7B, Bombo Rd,
Godino Palace

Justmor Inn, Gulu

P. O. Box 779
Plot 19 Coronation Road
Phone 256-900-285

Kabale Holiday Inn Ltd., Kabale

P. O. Box 866
Plot 174 Kabale Road

Kampala Inn, Kampala

P. O. Box 8640
Plot 92, Kira Road
Phone: 256-41-540-448
Alt. Phone: 256-77-443-594
Fax: 256-41-540-968

Katatumba Resort Hotel, Mbarara

P. O. Box 1177
Kabale Road
Phone: 256-0485-20152
Fax: 256-0485-21300

Katatumba Resort, Mbarara

P. O. Box 6968
Bwenkoma
Phone: +256-485-20152
Alt. Phone: +256-485-20152

Katatumba Suites, Kampala

P. O. Box 6968
2 Colville Street
Phone: +256-41-342913
Alt. Phone: +256-41-246441
Fax: +256-41-255288

Kihumuro Hills Road, Kabale

P. O. Box 475
Plot 17 Kisoro Road
Phone: 256-486-22131
Alt. Phone: 256-486-22440

Kiringa Guest House, Masaka

P. O. Box 1217
Bukoba Road
Phone: 256-481-20348

Kisoro Tourists Hotel, Kabale

P. O. Box 225
Kabale
Phone +256-486-30135

Lacan Pe Nino Central Bar & Lodging Gulu

P. O. Box 124
Plot 7 Lobwor Road

Lake Kutea Hotel, Lugazi

P. O. Box 159
Plot 70 Market Street
Phone 256-041-48258

Lake Nabugabo Holiday & Conf. Centre Resort, Masaka

P. O. Box 1760
Bukakata Road.

Lake View Hotel Ltd, Mbarara

P. O. Box 165
Fort Portal Road
Phone: 256-0485-20273
Alt. Phone: 256-0485-21397
Fax: 256-0485-21399

Lake View Regency, Kampala

Phone: 256-41-257814
Alt. Phone: 256-41-234903
Fax: 256-41-235658

Laston Hotel, Masaka

P. O. Box 243
Mutuba Garden
Phone 256-481-20209

L-Hotel Fiancee, Kampala

P. O. Box 4085
Plot 10, Channel Street,
UTC Village, Nakivubo
Phone 256-41-236144

Limu Hotel, Mbarara

P. O Box 443
Plot 49 Fort Portal Road

Lions Hotel Ltd, Kampala

P. O. Box 6751
Plot 18 Namirembe Rd.
Phone: 256-41-233934
Alt. Phone: 256-41-343490
Fax: 256-41-343682

Lira Hotel, Lira

P. O. Box 350
Plot 8/10 Erute Road
Phone: 256-473-20024

Lweza Training & Conference Centre, Kampala

P. O. Box 14123
Phone: 256-41-200210
Alt. Phone: 256-41-200012
Fax: 256-41-343757

Masindi Hotel Ltd., Masindi

P. O Box 11
Plot 22-34 Butiaba Road
Phone 256-465-20023

Mbarara Tralllevers Hotel, Mbarara

P. O Box 125
Plot 22 Fort Portal Road
Phone 256-0485-21233

Mbarara University Inn, Mbarara

P. O. Box 1410
Plot 9 Kabale Road
Phone 256-41-20337

Missouri Hotel, Kampala

P. O. Box 9492
Bombo Rd, Maganjo
Phone: 256-41-235901
Alt. Phone: 256-41-567726

Moroto Hotel, Moroto

Phone: 256-900-97
Fax: 256-900-235915

Motel Agip, Mbarara

P. O. Box 643,
Plot 36/48 Masaka Road
Phone 256-0485-21933

Mountains of the Moon Hotel, Fort Portal

P. O. Box 36
Plot 2, Nyaika Ave.
Phone 256-483-22513

Mt. Elgon Hotel (1997) Ltd., Mbale

P. O. Box 670
Plot 30 Masaba Road
Phone: 256-045-33454
Alt. Phone: 256-045-33612

Mt. Elgon View Hotel Ltd., Mbale

P. O. Box 967
Plot 5 Cathedral Avenue

Mt. Moroto Hotel, Moroto

Lorika Road
Phone 256-900-65

Muyenga Club, Kampala

P. O. Box 2255
Plot 1792, Kisugu
Phone: 256-41-266319
Fax: 256-41-230521

Mwaana Highway Hotel, Iganga

P. O Box 569
Main Street
Phone: 256-41-242595
Fax: 256-41-242595

Mwebaza Inn, Mukono

P. O Box 565
Jinja Road, Seeta
Phone 256-041-290706

Mweya Safari Lodge-Central Reservations, Kampala

P. O. Box 22827
Greenland Towers
Phone: 256-41-259390
Alt. Phone: 256-41-259394
Fax: 256-41-255277

Nakayiba Hilton Guest House, Masaka

P. O. Box 684
Nakayiba Kitovu Road
Phone 256-481-20537

Nakayima Hotel, Mubende

P. O. Box 175
Plot 34 Old Fort Portal Stree
Phone 256-464-4053

Namirembe Guest House, Kampala

P. O. Box 14127
Plot 1085, Will's Rd
Phone: 256-41-272071
Fax: 256-41-251925

New African Village, Entebbe

P. O. Box 271
Kampala Road
Phone 256-41-320835

New Bellevue Hotel, Jinja

P. O. Box 1730
Plot 4 Kutch Road
Phone 256-43-122731

New Gloria Hotel, Kampala

P. O. Box 9006
Plot 90, William Street
Phone: 256-41-257797
Alt. Phone: 256-41-257790
Fax: 256-41-234265

New Highland Hotel, Kabale

P. O. Box 95
Plot 1 Kazooba Road
Phone: 256-486-22175
Fax: 256-486-23742

Nobel Hotel Ltd, Kampala

P. O. Box 22689
Plot 23, Nakivubo Rd
Phone 256-41-345860

Nsamo Hotel, Hoima

P. O. Box 131
Plot 9/11 Old Fort Portal Road
Phone 256-465-40188

Pan Afrque Motel, Mbarara

P. O. Box 1069
Kabale Road
Phone 256-0485-236427

Paris Hotel, Kampala

P. O. Box 467
Plot 210, Mulago Hill Rd
Phone 256-41-540427

Peer Hotel Nateete, Kampala

P. O. Box 2747
Plot 1, Masaka Rd
Phone 256-41-270436

Pelikan Hotel Ltd., Mbarara

P. O. Box 1057
Plot 16/20 Bananuka Drive
Phone 256-045-20095

Pope Paul VI Memorial Comm. Centre, Kampala

P. O. Box 14326
Lugaga-Nabunya Rd.
Phone: 256-41-272189
Alt. Phone: 256-41-271133

Ranch on the Lake Hotel, Kampala

P. O. Box 6577
Kigo Off Entebbe Road
Phone: 256-41-200147
Alt. Phone: 256-41-344779
Fax: 256-41-200148

Resort Village, Mbale

P. O. Box 421
Plot 22 Maluku road
Phone: 256-045-33764

Riheka guest House, Mbarara

P. O. Box 234
Plot 1 Multi Road
Phone: 256-0485-21314

Roadmaster Hotel, Kampala

P. O. Box 8188
Hoima Rd, Nakulabye
Phone 256-41-532989

Rock Hotel Tororo Ltd., Tororo

P. O. Box 293
Osukulu Road
Phone: 256-045-44654
Alt. Phone: 256-045-44655
Fax: 256-045-44458

Rondovels Hotel Rukungiri, Rukungiri

P. O. Box 116
Off Ntungamo road
Phone 256-486-42598

Royal Hotel, Kampala

P. O. Box 21985
Plot 35, Luwuum Street
Phone: 256-41-348399
Alt. Phone: 256-41-348400

Rwezori View Guest House, Fort Portal

P. O. Box 790
Plot 15 Lower Kiiza Road
Phone 256-483-22102

Rwizi Arch Hotel, Mbarara

P. O. Box 91
Fort Portal Road
Phone: 256-0485-20821
Fax: 256-0485-20402

Sad Hotel ltd., Kasese

P. O. Box 70
Plot 27-31 Stanley Road
Phone 256483-44139

Safari TransAfrique, Kampala

P. O. Box 7666
Plot 7 parliament Avenue
Phone: 256-41-250695
Fax: 256-41-233363

SafariLand Park & Paradise Lodge, Mbarara

P. O. Box 1512
Kabale Road
Phone 26-0485-21692

Salem Uganda, Mbale

P. O. Box 1558
Kumi Road
Phone: 256-045-33601
Fax: 256-045-33601

Samalien Properties Ltd., Kampala

Phone: 256-41-543049
Alt. Phone: 256-41-341023
Fax: 256-41-543048

Sanyu Hotel, Mbarara

P. O. Box 266
Plot 5 Masaka Road
Phone 256-0485-20089

Sayona Hotel, Kampala

P. O. Box 21985
Nkurumah Rd.

Silver Springs, Kampala

P. O. Box 734
Plot 76/78, Port Bell Rd Luzira
Phone: 256-41-221231
Fax: 256-41-236361

Skyblue Motel, Kabale

P. O. Box 741
Kabale Road
Phone 256-486-22154

Skyline Hotel, Kabale

P. O. Box 78
Plot 4 Kabale Road
Phone 256-486-24071

Sophies Motel, Entebbe

P. O. Box 730
Plot 3. 5 Alice Reef Road
Phone: 256-41-321-370
Alt. Phone: 256-41-320-885
Fax: 256-41-320-897

Soroti Hotel Ltd., Soroti

P. O. Box 1
Plot 13-16 Serere Road
Phone: 256-045-61269
Fax: 256-045-61269

Sports View Hotel, Kampala

P. O. Box 7,
Jinja Rd Kireka
Phone: 256-41-286013
Alt. Phone: 256-41-285118
Fax: 256-41-342041

Ssese Islands Beach Hotel, Kalangala

Kalangala,
Buggala Island
Phone: +256-41-220065
Alt. Phone: +256-41-505098
Fax: +256-41-220242

Sunrise Hotel Tororo, Tororo

P. O. Box 267
Plot 1 Tague Avenue
Phone 256-045-44665

Sunrise Inn, Mbale

P. O. Box 2607
Plot 45 Nankhuka Road
Phone: 256-045-33090
Fax: 256-045-33865

Sunset Hotel International Ltd., Jinja

P. O. Box 156
Plot 16/17 Kiira Road
Phone: 256-43-120575
Alt. Phone: 256-43-120194
Fax: 256-43-120741

Terrance Hotel, Kampala

P. O. Box 5380
Hoima Rd
Phone 256-41-542990

The Hotel Diplomate, Kampala

P. O. Box 3953
William Kalema Drive, Muyenga
Phone: 256-41-267625
Alt. Phone: 256-41-267255
Fax: 256-41-267655

Timton Hotel Ltd., Jinja

P. O. Box 341
Plot 15 Jackson Crescent
Phone: 256-43-120278
Fax: 256-43-121322

Tourist Hotel, Kampala

P. O. Box 7035
Market Street, Nakasero
Phone: 256-41-251471
Alt. Phone: 256-41-251472
Fax: 256-41-235345

Tourist Hotel, Kampala

P. O. Box 7036 Kampala
Plot 9 Market Street
Phone: 256-41-251471
Alt. Phone: 256-41-251473
Fax: 256-41-251472

Tourist Motel, Kampala

P. O. Box 4642
Plot 1/3 Jinja road
Phone 256-41-257426

Town View Hotel, Lira

P. O. Box 201
Plot 1A Bala Road
Phone 256-473-20121

Travellers Choice, Jinja

P. O. Box 508
Jinja Road, Seeta
Phone 256-43-290175

Ulrika Guest House, Entebbe

P. O. Box 91
Gogonya Kisubi
Phone 256-41-320909

Victoria Inn, Entebbe

P. O. Box 92
Plot 29 Mpigi Road
Phone 256-41-321214

Visitors Hotel, Kabale

P. O. Box 123
Plot 5 Kabale Road
Phone 256-486-22239

Wash & Wills Country Home, Mbale

P. O Box 1327
Plot 37 Mbiro Road
Phone: 256-045-35264
Fax: 256-045-34173

Western Hotel, Mbarara

P. O. Box 1348
Plot 8 Bulemba Road
Phone 256-0485-20653

WestLand International, Mbarara

P. O. Box 905
Plot 9 Bananuka Drive
Phone 256-0485-20044

White Horse Inn, Kabale

P. O. Box 11
Plot 25 Rwamaga
Phone: 256-486-23336/7
Alt. Phone: 256-486-23399
Fax: 256-486-23717

White View Restaurant & Lodge, Luwero

P. O. Box 14
Gulu Road

Wooden Hotel, Fort Portal

P. O. Box 560
Plot 4, Kyebambe Rd
Phone 256-483-22566-

Yovani Hotel, Kampala

P. O. Box 8540
Plot 25, Namiremb Rd-
Nakulabye
Phone: 256-41-258389
Alt. Phone: 256-41-258525
Fax: 256-41-285535

Internet Cafes

Bonus Enterprises, Kampala

P.O Box 11132,
Plot 4 Colville Street,
Ebenezer House
Phone : +256-41-231323
Alt. Phone: +256-77-471729
Fax: +256-41-231323

Cheeky Monkey WebCafe, Kampala

P.O Box 10385,
Plot 12 William Street 2nd Floor
opp. Standard Chartered Bank
Phone: +256-77-444956
Alt. Phone: +256-75-444956

Click Computer Centre, Kampala

P.O Box 11625,
Uganda House Shopping Arcade,
Kampala Road
Phone: +256-77-411866

Cyber Click Café, Kampala

Wilson Road,
Plot 8 Bhatial Building,
Phone: +256-75-748680
Alt. Phone: +256-77-501848

Cyber World Café, Kampala

P.O Box 3750,
Plot 83 / 85 Park Royal Building,
Kampala Road
Phone: +256-41-340491

Cyberspot Café, Kampala

Kampala Road,
Plot 64 Makerere Hill Road
Phone: +256-77-451645
Alt. Phone: +256-77-514388

Famous Internet Café Kampala

Bombo Road
Phone: +256-77-491-043

Franscom Internet Café, Kampala

P.O Box 12421,
Pioneer Mall Shop ,
Johnson Street
Phone: +256-77-414151
Alt. Phone: +256-77-434305

Lotus Club5 Café, Kampala

Complex Hall,
Makerere University
Phone: +256-77-567010

Lotus Internet Café, Kampala

Ben Kiwanuka Street,
Plot 72, Shop N9 Bhatia Towers
Phone: +256-41-349266

Moonlight Cyber Café, Kampala

P.O Box 12421 Kampala Uganda,
1st Floor Room No. 109

Kalungi Plaza Wiliam Street

Phone: 256-071-809363

Net Café, Kampala

P. O Box 1262,
Communications House
4th Floor Colville Street
Phone: 256-77-489-965

Star 2 Uganda Ltd, Kampala

Bombo Road, opp. Hotel Equatorial
Phone: 256-41-232-204
Alt. Phone: 256-77-404-282

The Peternet Café, Kampala

P.O Box 245,
Pioneer Mansions Building
Upper Luwum Street
Phone: +256-77-491142
Alt. Phone: +256-77-505686

Trans.com, Kampala

Kampala Road,
Pioneer Mall Shop No.2
Phone: 256-41-258-481
Fax: 256-41-258-481

Uganda Management Institute, Kampala

P.O Box 20131,
Plot 44 /52 Jinja Road,
Lugogo
Phone: +256-41-345990
Alt. Phone: +256-41-259312
Fax: +256-41-259-314

Niteclubs & Cinemas

Ange Nior Discotheque

Plot 77a, First Street
Industrial Area
Tel: 230190

Cine Afrique

Plot 70, Kampala Road
Tel: 236379

Cineplex Cinema

Plot 10, Wilson Road
Kampala,
Tel: 347713, 348055

e-mail: cineplex@africaonline. co. ug

Club Obligatto

Old Port Bell Road

Club Silk

Plot 15/17, Second Street
Tel: 345362, 250907
Fax: 345372

The Viper Room

Equatoria Hotel
Tel: 250780, 077 200380
Fax: 232364